Editorial Project Manager
Lorin E. Klistoff, M.A.

Editor-in-Chief
Sharon Coan, M.S. Ed.

Illustrator
Howard Chaney
Renée Christine Yates

Cover Artist
Barb Lorseyedi

Art Coordinator
Kevin Barnes

Imaging
James Edward Grace
Alfred Lau

Product Manager
Phil Garcia

Publisher
Mary D. Smith, M.S. Ed.

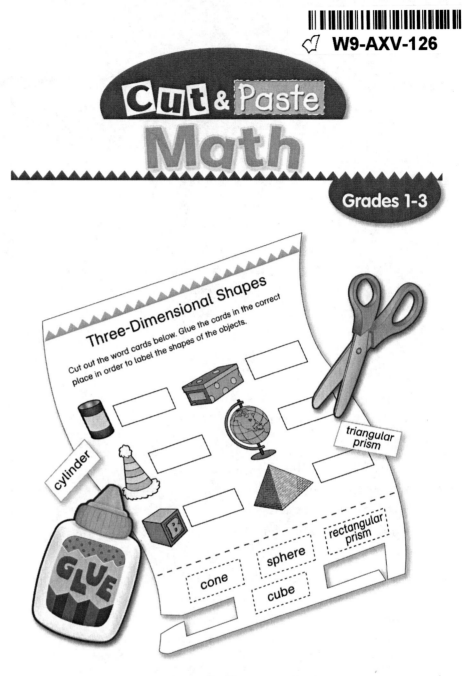

W9-AXV-126

Cut & Paste Math

Grades 1-3

Author

Jodene Lynn Smith, M.A.

Teacher Created Resources, Inc.
12621 Western Avenue
Garden Grove, CA 92841
www.teachercreated.com

ISBN: 978-0-7439-3708-5

©2003 Teacher Created Resources, Inc.
Reprinted, 2016

Made in U.S.A.

Table of Contents

Introduction

Cut & Paste Math was designed to help the classroom teacher teach and reinforce math concepts and skills. The contents of the book provide a variety of ways to cover math content while maintaining student interest.

The book is divided into five main sections. At the beginning of each section is an introduction to the section that includes suggested ideas and activities to use while teaching concepts covered within that section. Most of the ideas can be adapted to be presented as whole-class lessons, small group reinforcements, or even math center activities. The ideas are meant to be a resource for teachers as they teach these content area skills.

Following the introduction for each section are activity pages that are directly related to math concepts and skills. Each of the pages has been designed in a cut-and-paste format. After cutting out word cards, numeral cards, or picture cards at the bottom of the page, students will use those cards in order to complete the page. By manipulating the cards, students are able to try a variety of possibilities before gluing the cards down for their final answers. The pages vary in the tasks that students are asked to perform. In some cases, they are asked to glue the correct answer to a problem. In other cases, students are asked to sort or categorize pictures according to math concepts. In all cases, students are asked to interact in a meaningful way with the content of the topic on which they are working.

The book has been designed so that it is organized and easy to use. Teachers will find the suggested activities useful for teaching math content. Students will find the cut-and-paste activities a fun way to practice math concepts. Above all, math content is made available in a way that requires students to interact with it.

Number Sense

Suggested Activities

Below are suggested activities that can be used throughout the unit of study.

- This game can be played with 2–5 players. Gather together a 100's chart, one die, and objects that can be used as markers. The first student roles the die. The student moves his or her marker on the hundreds chart according to the number shown on the die. Then it is the next student's turn. Play continues until the first student has reached 100. The game can be modified in a variety of ways to reflect the concepts on which you are currently working. For example, provide two dice and have students add the numbers together or subtract the numbers to determine how many spaces to move.

- Provide strips of paper 3" x 18" (8 cm x 46 cm), an ink pad, and some rubber stamps. Have students use the stamps to create a line of stamped images. Then, students can go back with a pencil or crayon and label the images. Students can use numerals, numeral names, or even ordinal numbers. Create even longer lines of stamped images with a longer piece of paper or by taping together several students' papers and label the images by counting by 10's, 5's, or 2's.

- Line students up for recess a few minutes early. Call out that the class should do an "Ordinal Number Count Off." Go down the line pointing to students as they call off their position in line using ordinal numbers. The student at the head of the line should say, "First." Students continue counting until the last student has been reached. This is a fun way to pass the time when your class is lined up and waiting for an event to happen, for example, waiting for lunch to be served, etc.

- Write the ordinal number words on a clothespin. Create a clothesline by tying a piece of string to two chairs and separating the chairs about 3 feet. Students must clip the clothespins on the clothesline in the correct ordinal number order.

- Create number lines for practicing counting by 2's, 5's, and 10's. Have students think of objects that come in multiples of the number by which you will be counting. For example, if you will be creating a number line counting by 2's, students might come up with the idea of mittens. Students then either draw a pair of mittens or they can get creative and cut the mittens out of construction paper, fabric, or wallpaper. Glue each student's pair of mittens on a long strip of butcher paper or cash register tape. Number each of the mittens. Make the numbers that are multiples of two stand out in some way such as by making them larger, glittering them, or writing them in another color. Then, once the number line is hung, students can easily see a faster way of counting all of the mittens on the number line. Practice counting the objects by two as a class.

Two by Two

Directions: Cut out the numeral cards at the bottom of the page. Glue them in the correct places in order to count by twos.

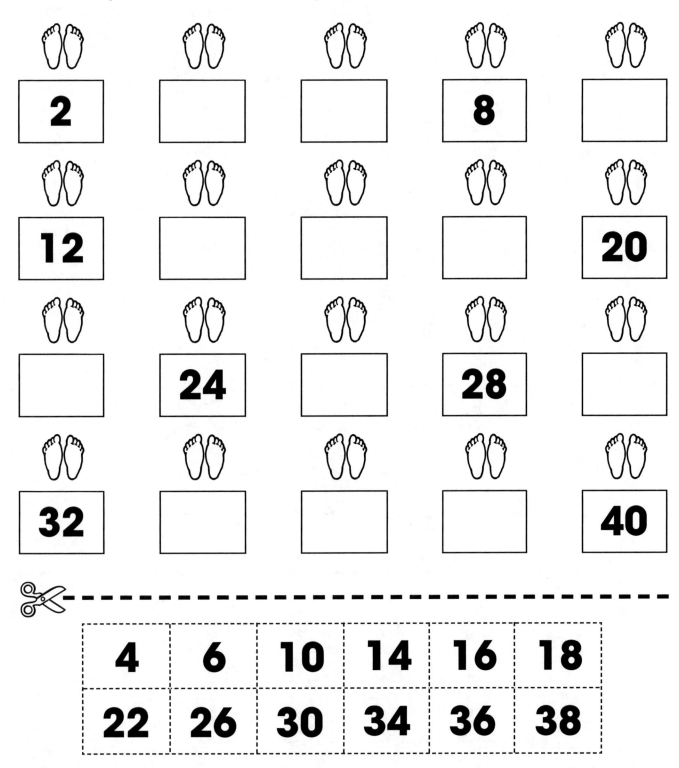

Counting by ?

Directions: Cut out the numeral cards at the bottom of the page. For each problem, determine if the pattern is counting by twos, fives, or tens. Glue the correct numeral cards in the blanks in order to complete the patterned counting.

1. 40, 50, ☐, 70, ☐, 90, 100

2. 5, 10, 15, ☐, 25, ☐, 35

3. 2, 4, ☐, 8, 10, ☐, 14

4. 20, ☐, 40, ☐, 60, 70, 80

5. ☐, 20, 25, 30, ☐, 40, 45

6. 26, 28, 30, ☐, 34, 36, ☐

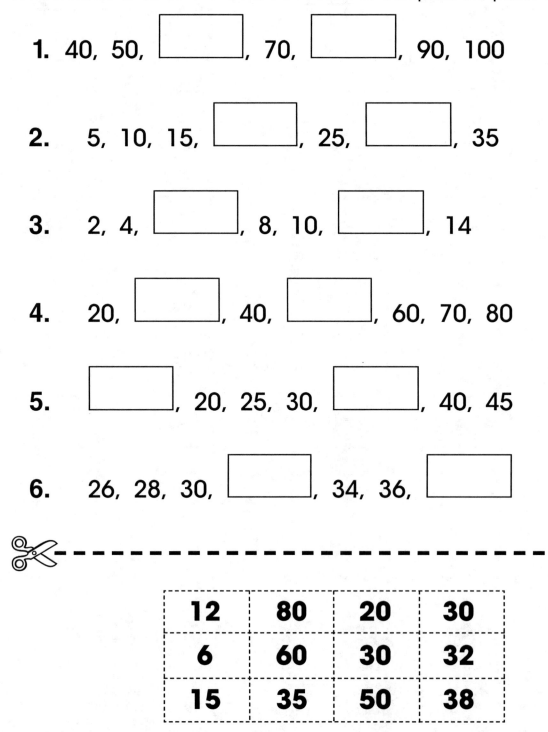

12	80	20	30
6	60	30	32
15	35	50	38

Make It True

Directions: Cut out the numeral cards at the bottom of the page. Glue the cards in the boxes below to make each statement true.

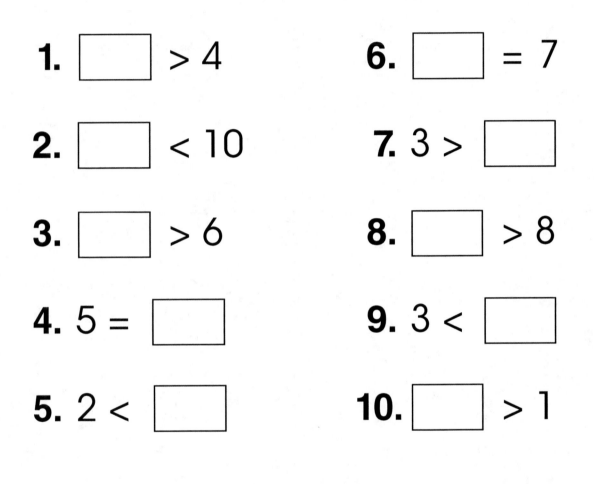

1. ☐ > 4

2. ☐ < 10

3. ☐ > 6

4. 5 = ☐

5. 2 < ☐

6. ☐ = 7

7. 3 > ☐

8. ☐ > 8

9. 3 < ☐

10. ☐ > 1

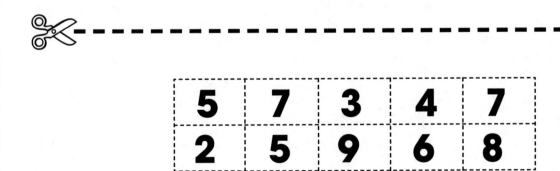

5	7	3	4	7
2	5	9	6	8

Greater Than, Less Than, or Equal

Directions: Cut out the sign cards at the bottom of the page. Use them in the problems below to make each true.

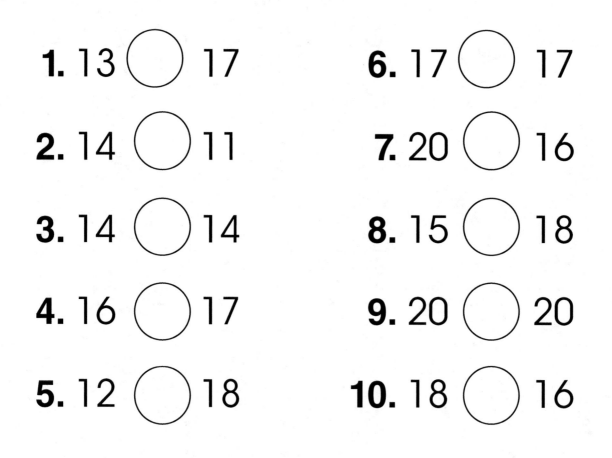

1. 13 ◯ 17   **6.** 17 ◯ 17

2. 14 ◯ 11   **7.** 20 ◯ 16

3. 14 ◯ 14   **8.** 15 ◯ 18

4. 16 ◯ 17   **9.** 20 ◯ 20

5. 12 ◯ 18   **10.** 18 ◯ 16

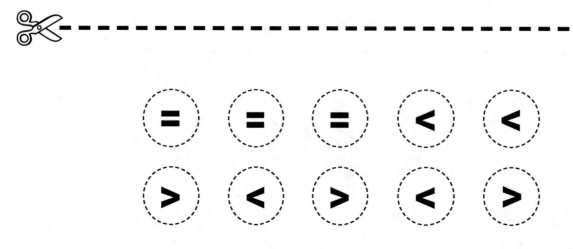

True or False?

Directions: Cut out the numeral statements at the bottom of the page. Decide if each statement is true or false. Glue each card in the correct column below.

TRUE	FALSE

✂ -

76 > 72	**21 > 28**	**91 > 89**	**67 < 61**
84 = 84	**63 < 67**	**82 < 79**	**33 < 38**
46 > 48	**49 > 51**	**43 > 36**	**73 < 71**

Tens and Ones

Directions: Cut out the numeral cards at the bottom of the page. Look at the ones and tens rods below. Determine the number being shown in each picture. Glue the correct numeral card next to each picture.

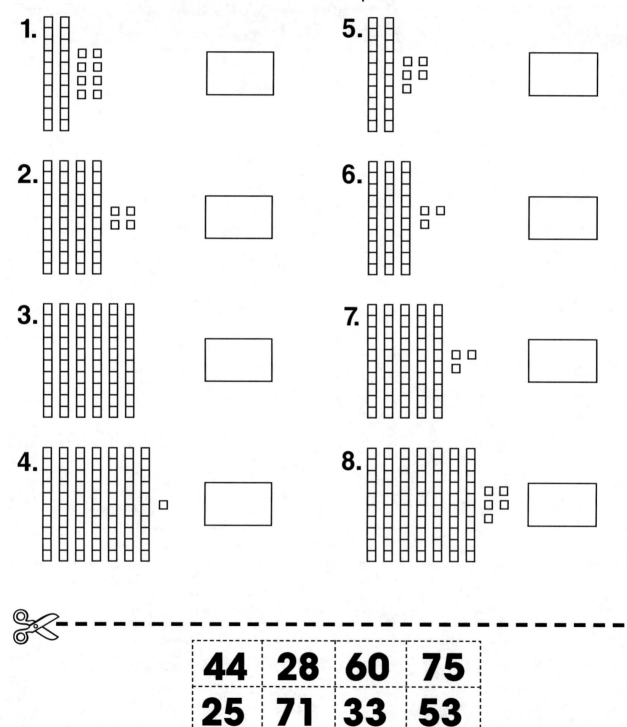

1.

5.

2.

6.

3.

7.

4.

8.

44	28	60	75
25	71	33	53

Show the Numeral

Directions: Cut out the picture cards at the bottom of the page. Use the pictures to illustrate the numeral shown below.

1.

124

2.

237

3.

241

4.

173

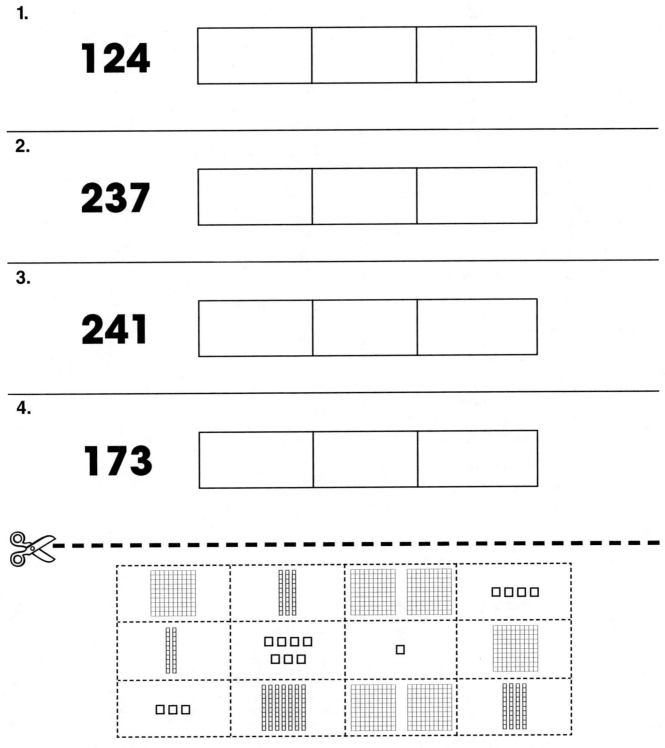

Make a Number

Directions: Cut out the numeral cards at the bottom of the page. Read the clues below in order to make the number stated. Glue the numeral cards in the correct places.

1. Make a numeral that has . . .
   a 6 in the ones place,
   a 9 in the tens place,
   and a 4 in the hundreds place.

2. Make a numeral that has . . .
   a 2 in the ones place,
   a 7 in the tens place,
   and a 3 in the hundreds place.

3. Make a numeral that has . . .
   a 8 in the ones place,
   a 4 in the tens place,
   and a 1 in the hundreds place.

4. Make a numeral that has . . .
   a 0 in the ones place,
   a 5 in the tens place,
   and a 3 in the hundreds place.

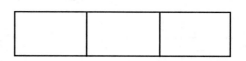

5. Make a numeral that has . . .
   a 9 in the ones place,
   a 0 in the tens places,
   and a 2 in the hundreds place.

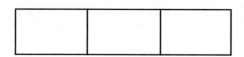

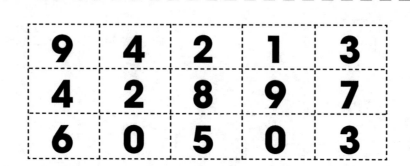

1 More

Directions: Read the sentences. Glue one more of the same object in the picture. Count how many there are.

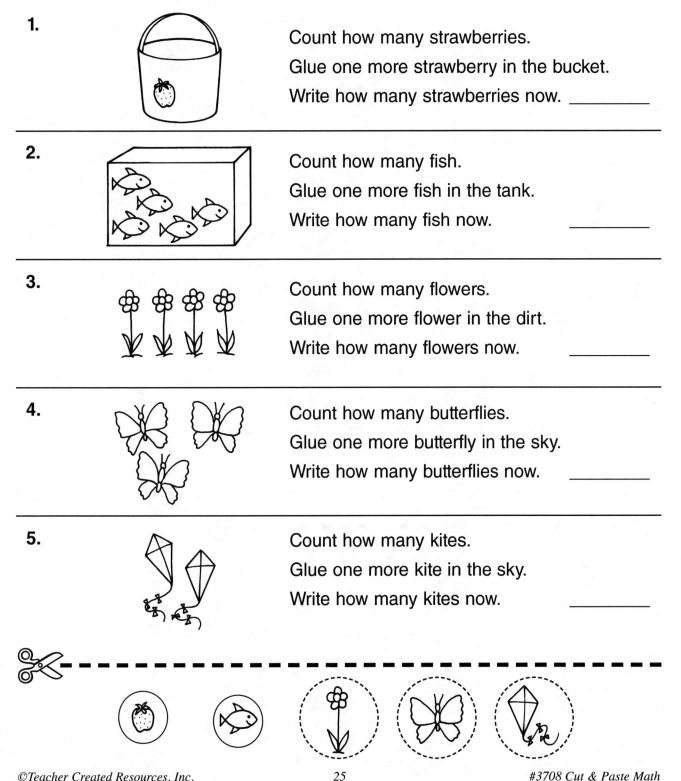

1.

Count how many strawberries.

Glue one more strawberry in the bucket.

Write how many strawberries now. _____

2.

Count how many fish.

Glue one more fish in the tank.

Write how many fish now. _____

3.

Count how many flowers.

Glue one more flower in the dirt.

Write how many flowers now. _____

4.

Count how many butterflies.

Glue one more butterfly in the sky.

Write how many butterflies now. _____

5.

Count how many kites.

Glue one more kite in the sky.

Write how many kites now. _____

1 More, 1 Less

Directions: Cut out the numeral cards at the bottom of the page. Glue the cards in the correct places to show one more (box on the right) and one less (box on the left) than the numeral shown in the center box.

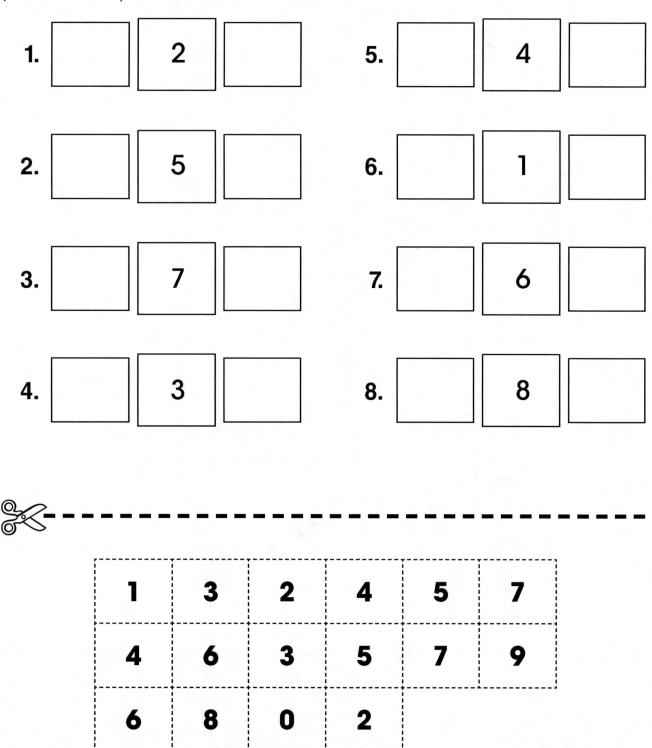

10 More, 10 Less

Directions: Cut out the numeral cards at the bottom of the page. Glue the cards in the correct places in order to show ten more or ten less than the numerals shown.

# Number	+10 Ten More
5	
23	
47	
54	
86	
90	

# Number	-10 Ten Less
30	
43	
57	
64	
71	
95	

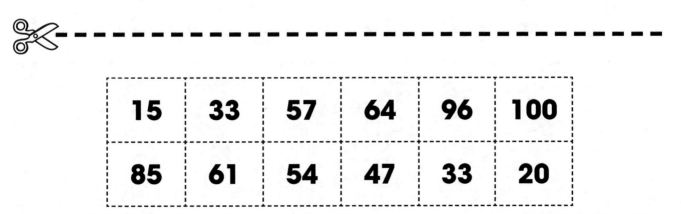

15	33	57	64	96	100
85	61	54	47	33	20

Money in My Wallet

Directions: Cut out the coins at the bottom of the page. Glue the coins in the wallets so that each wallet has the amount shown on the wallet.

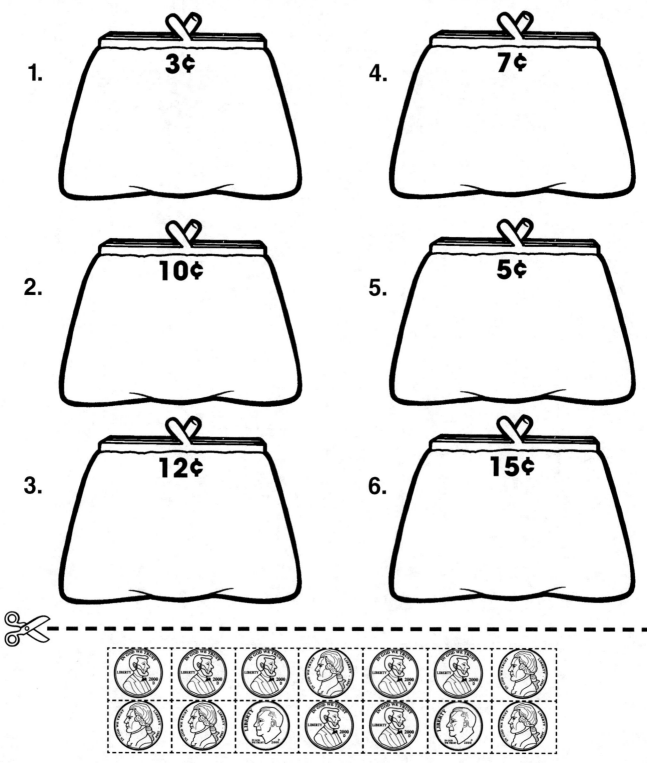

1. 3¢

4. 7¢

2. 10¢

5. 5¢

3. 12¢

6. 15¢

How Much Does It Cost?

Directions: Cut out the picture cards at the bottom of the page. Count the coins at the top of the page. Match the picture card whose price tag shows the same amount of money as the coins counted. Glue the picture cards in the correct places.

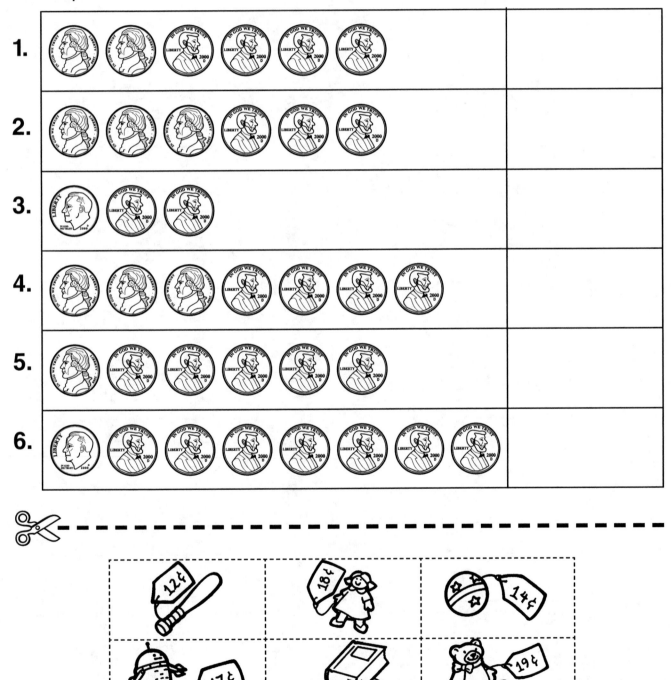

Make Change

Directions: Cut out the cards at the bottom of the page. For each problem, you pay the cashier $2.00 for the item shown. How much change will you receive? Glue the card showing the correct amount of change you will receive next to each item.

You Pay: $2.00

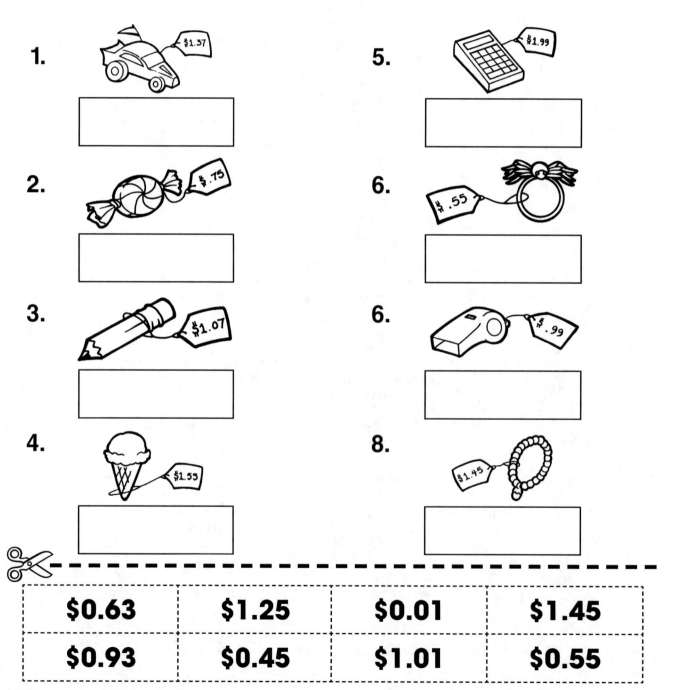

1. $1.57

2. $.75

3. $1.07

4. $1.55

5. $1.99

6. $.55

6. $.99

8. $1.45

| $0.63 | $1.25 | $0.01 | $1.45 |
| $0.93 | $0.45 | $1.01 | $0.55 |

Computation

Suggested Activities

Below are suggested activities that can be used throughout the unit of study.

- Gather a piece of chalk and two beanbags. On the carpet or cement outside, draw 3–5 circles in the shape of a target. Label each circle with a numeral. Students must stand at a designated place and toss the two beanbags. Students must look at the numerals from the circles where the beanbags landed and add them together. Once the sum has been named, and the team agrees that the sum is correct, the student receives one point. Play continues, alternating students tossing the beanbags until one player reaches 10 points. For a challenge, add an extra beanbag and have students practice adding with three addends. The game can be used for multiplication, too.

- Provide two dice for each group of students and a piece of paper. Students will create their own addition or subtraction number sentences. Students should take turns rolling the dice to determine numerals to use as addends. After the dice have been rolled, students should use the number of dots on the dice as the addends in their number sentence. Once the number sentence has been written down and a sum or difference determined, another student may roll the dice. Students should continue until they reach a predetermined number of problems. This activity can be used in order to practice multiplication for older students, too.

- Demonstrate to students just how much we use computation in our everyday lives. Each time you come across a computation you need to do, include the class in figuring out the answer. For example, ask the class questions such as, "There are 20 students in the class. Each child needs two pieces of black paper for the art project. How many pieces of paper do I need in all?" Students enjoy helping to figure out these type of real-world problems. It is highly beneficial to show them applications of the computation they are learning to do.

- Dominoes provide a great way to practice computation. Obtain some dominoes. Lay the dominoes face down on the table. Students can select one domino to use in writing number sentences. Count the number of dots on the top half of the domino and the number of dots on the bottom half of the domino and use those two numbers as the addends when writing the number sentence. Before the students place the domino back in the pile, they should turn the domino around in order to write the related fact. Use dominos when practicing multiplication, too.

- Create some clothespin games for students to use to practice basic facts. Write facts (addition, subtraction, multiplication, or division) down both sides of a piece of index paper. Write the numeral that would answer each problem on both sides of a clothespin. Place the clothespins and the problem card together in a small, plastic bag. When a student wants to practice the facts on the card, he pours out the contents of the bag and clips the clothespins to the card to correctly answer each problem.

- Write your lunch count in the form of a number sentence each day. One addend should be the number of students that will be buying lunch. The other addend should be the number of students that brought their lunches from home. Be sure to include the sum.

Computation *(cont.)*

Suggested Activities *(cont.)*

- Gather or make two-color counters. The counters should be one color on one side and another color on the other side. Students pick up the counters, shake them in their hands, and release them on the table. Students then use the colors that are face-up on the counters to create a number sentence. For example, if two red counters are showing and four yellow counters are showing, the student would write the problem: $2 + 4 = 6$. Once the student has written down the number sentence, he or she picks up the counters and repeats. Students should continue play until a predetermined number of number sentences have been written down.

- Save the grocery store ads that come in the mail. Provide them for students to use in writing their own problems. Students should cut out several food items from the ads, write a story problem about the food items, and then show their number sentence that corresponds.

- Demonstrate that you can add in any order (or multiply) by creating cards with addition facts written at the bottom of each card. Draw dots or pictures above each addend to represent the numbers being added. For example, if the problem is $2 + 1 = 3$, students can draw two dots above the numeral 2 and 1 dot above the numeral 1. Then, turn the card upside down and have students write down the new addition number sentence by writing $1 + 2 = 3$. The dots will already be drawn; the number sentence will simply have to be written down. Students will be able to see that the number of dots or objects does not change just because the addends are reversed in their order, thus the sum is the same when you "add in any order."

- Provide students with rubber stamps or stickers for them to use in illustrating multiplication number sentences. Students can either stamp first, then determine the number sentence based on what they have stamped; or they can determine the number sentence and then use the stamps to illustrate it. Have students simply illustrate a number sentence or have them write a word problem that goes with their illustration. This activity can also be used to illustrate addition or subtraction number sentences, too.

- Teach multiplication through the use of arrays. Students illustrate the multiplication problem with lines representing the numbers in the problem. The first numeral being multiplied is represented by an equal number of vertical lines. The second numeral being multiplied is represented by an equal number of horizontal lines that cross the vertical lines. The points where the lines cross can be counted up to show the product. For example, the problem $2 \times 5 = 10$ would look like this as an array:

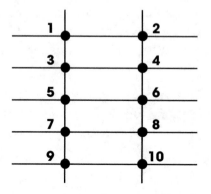

Illustrate the Problem

Directions: Cut out the picture cards at the bottom of the page. Glue the picture cards in the correct places in order to illustrate the number sentences written below. Write the sum of each problem.

1.

    2 + 1 =

4.

    5 + 1 =

2.

    4 + 0 =

5.

    5 + 2 =

3.

    2 + 3 =

6.

    3 + 4 =

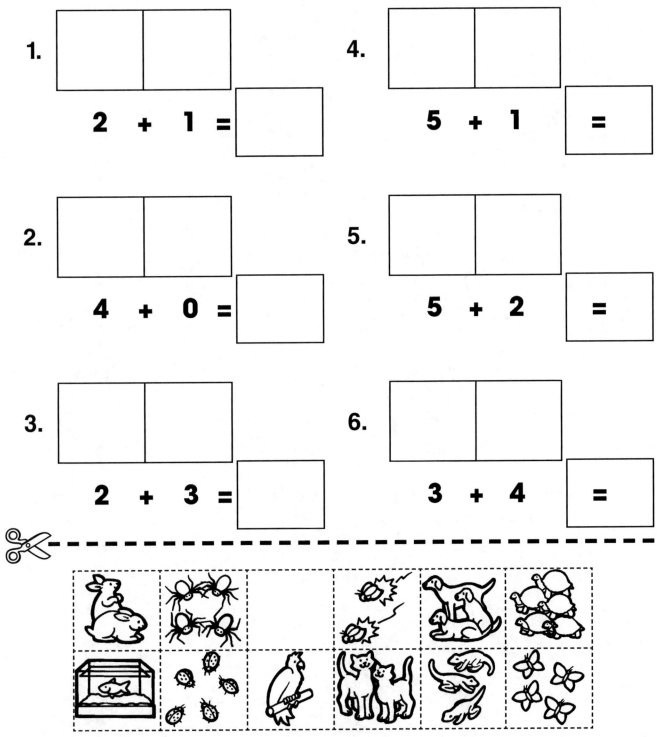

Flower Power

Directions: Cut out the flower petals at the bottom of the page. Glue the petals on the flower that shows the sum for the problem on the petal.

Make Your Own Problem

Directions: Cut out the number word cards at the bottom of the page. Create your own word problem by gluing the word cards in the sentences below. Draw a picture of your problem in the box provided. Then, write a number sentence to go with your word problem.

1. Ken has [_____]. Mandi gives him [_____] more. How many does Ken have in all? _____	Draw
2. Miguel found [_____]. Then he found [_____] more. How many does Miguel have altogether? _____	Draw
3. Pei has [_____]. Felix gave him [_____] more. How many does Pei have in all? _____	Draw
4. Jenny saw [_____]. Then she saw [_____] more. How many did Jenny see altogether? _____	Draw

✂ -

six	one	two flowers	three hats
five	two	four pencils	five bugs

The Perfect Nest

Directions: Cut out the nests at the bottom of the page. Glue the nests under the eggs in order to show the correct sums.

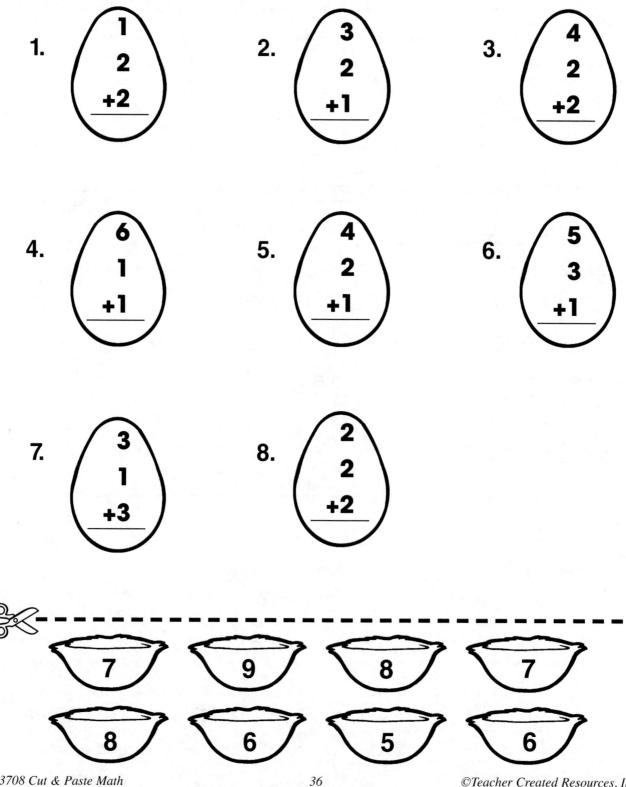

1.
```
  1
  2
+2
```

2.
```
  3
  2
+1
```

3.
```
  4
  2
+2
```

4.
```
  6
  1
+1
```

5.
```
  4
  2
+1
```

6.
```
  5
  3
+1
```

7.
```
  3
  1
+3
```

8.
```
  2
  2
+2
```

7   9   8   7

8   6   5   6

Mouse Food

Directions: Cut out the pieces of cheese at the bottom of the page. Glue the pieces of cheese below the mice in order to show the correct sums.

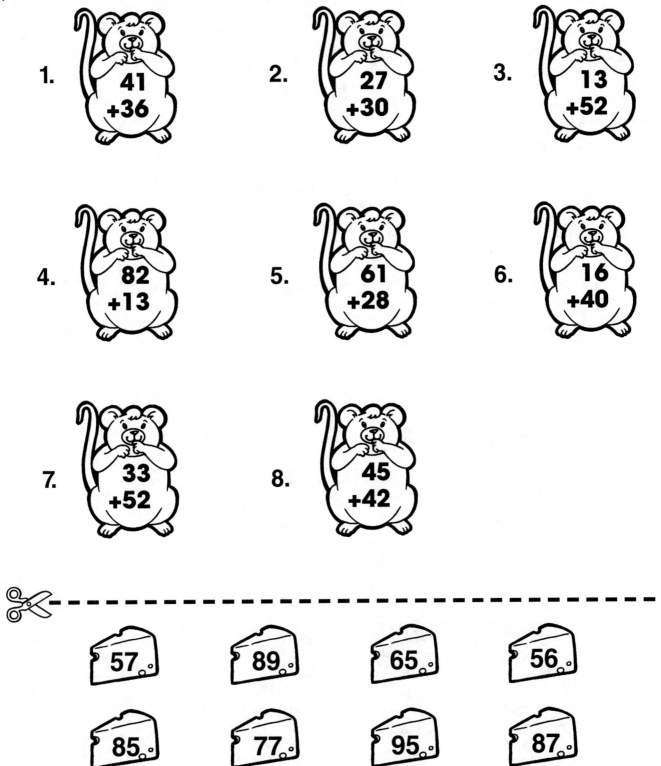

1. 41
   +36

2. 27
   +30

3. 13
   +52

4. 82
   +13

5. 61
   +28

6. 16
   +40

7. 33
   +52

8. 45
   +42

57   89   65   56

85   77   95   87

Bee Hives

Directions: Cut out the bees at the bottom of the page. Glue the bees in the correct places in order to show the sums for the problems on the hives.

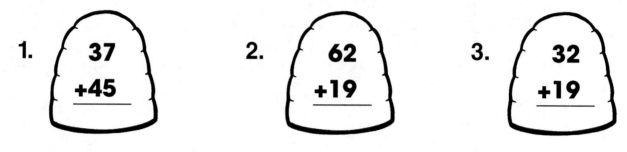

1.
```
 37
+45
___
```

2.
```
 62
+19
___
```

3.
```
 32
+19
___
```

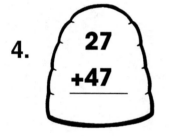 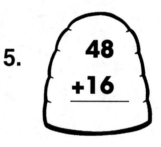 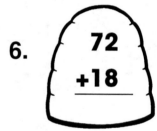

4.
```
 27
+47
___
```

5.
```
 48
+16
___
```

6.
```
 72
+18
___
```

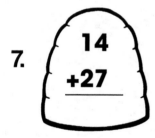 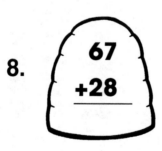

7.
```
 14
+27
___
```

8.
```
 67
+28
___
```

82 81 74 95

41 64 90 51

Show the Picture

Directions: Cut out the picture cards at the bottom of the page. Glue the pictures in the correct places in order to illustrate the subtraction number sentences below.

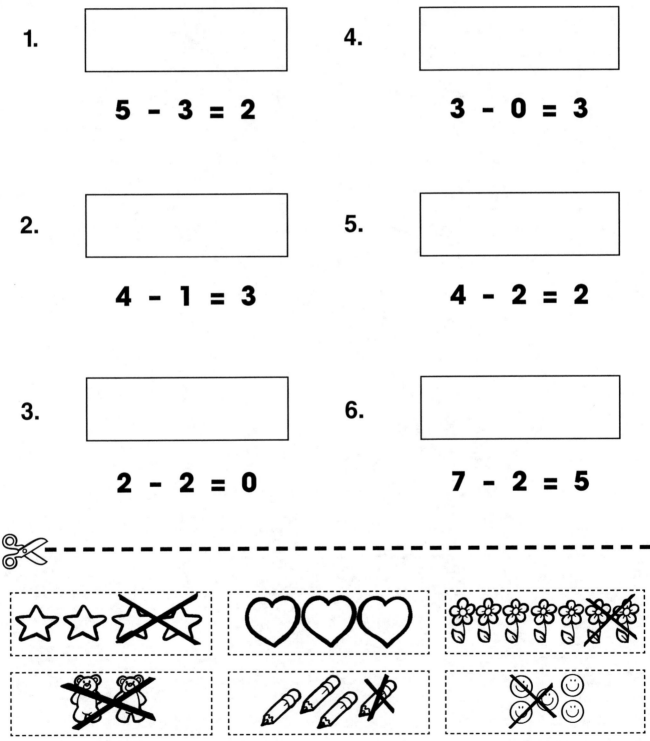

1.

5 - 3 = 2

4.

3 - 0 = 3

2.

4 - 1 = 3

5.

4 - 2 = 2

3.

2 - 2 = 0

6.

7 - 2 = 5

Birds of a Feather

Directions: Cut out the feathers at the bottom of the page. Glue the feathers on the turkeys below in order to show the difference for the problems on the turkey feathers.

Make the Number Sentence

Directions: Cut out the numeral cards at the bottom of the page. Read each word problem. Use the numeral cards to create the correct number sentence for each problem.

1. Five birds sat on a fence. Two birds flew away. How many birds were left?

2. Seven kids were swimming in a pool. Three kids got out of the pool. How many kids were left?

3. Three boys were riding their bikes. All of the boys had to go home. How many boys were left?

4. Mom had six cookies. She gave two cookies to me. Now how many cookies does mom have?

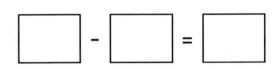

5. I had nine flowers in the garden. I picked five flowers to bring in the house. Now how many flowers are in the garden?

6. Mark had four apples. He ate one apple every day for three days. How many apples does he have left?

0	3	3	7	3	4
6	5	2	3	4	4
5	2	4	9	3	1

Give It a Bottom

Directions: Cut out the bottoms of the cupcakes below the dashed line. Glue the bottoms in the correct places to show the differences for the problems below.

1. 79 −23

2. 42 −10

3. 38 −17

4. 65 −32

5. 92 −51

6. 88 −70

7. 25 −13

8. 57 −16

41   32   21   18

41   56   12   33

Two Scoops

Directions: Cut out the cones at the bottom of the page. Glue the cones in the correct places to show the differences for the problems below.

1.
$$\begin{array}{r} 73 \\ -17 \\ \hline \end{array}$$

2.
$$\begin{array}{r} 45 \\ -26 \\ \hline \end{array}$$

3.
$$\begin{array}{r} 38 \\ -29 \\ \hline \end{array}$$

4.
$$\begin{array}{r} 91 \\ -73 \\ \hline \end{array}$$

5.
$$\begin{array}{r} 64 \\ -37 \\ \hline \end{array}$$

6.
$$\begin{array}{r} 57 \\ -18 \\ \hline \end{array}$$

7.
$$\begin{array}{r} 88 \\ -39 \\ \hline \end{array}$$

8.
$$\begin{array}{r} 74 \\ -67 \\ \hline \end{array}$$

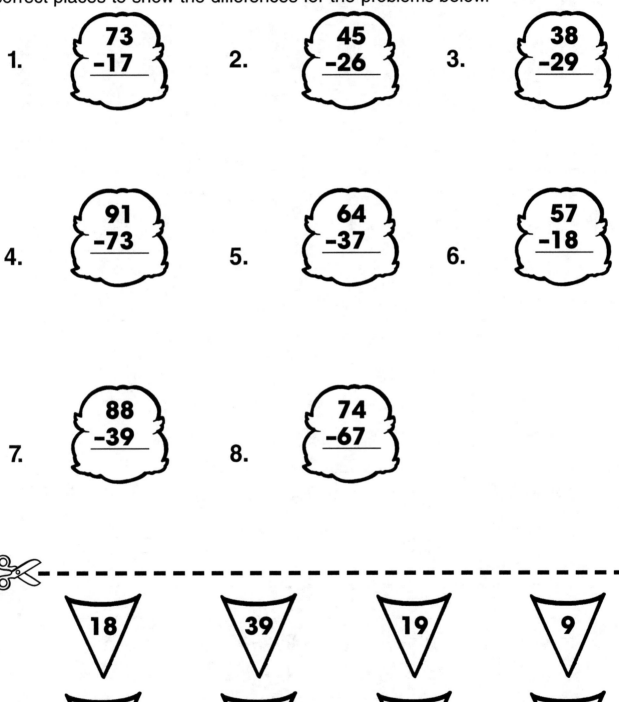

18   39   19   9

7   56   49   27

Find the Families

Directions: Cut out the pairs of number sentences at the bottom of the page. Glue them in the correct places to show fact families.

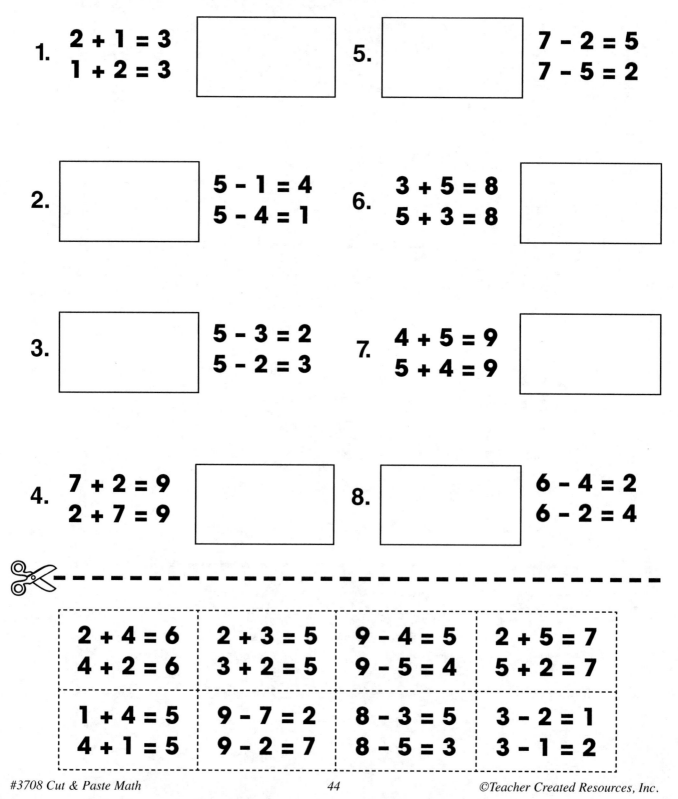

1.
2 + 1 = 3
1 + 2 = 3

5.
7 - 2 = 5
7 - 5 = 2

2.
5 - 1 = 4
5 - 4 = 1

6.
3 + 5 = 8
5 + 3 = 8

3.
5 - 3 = 2
5 - 2 = 3

7.
4 + 5 = 9
5 + 4 = 9

4.
7 + 2 = 9
2 + 7 = 9

8.
6 - 4 = 2
6 - 2 = 4

2 + 4 = 6	2 + 3 = 5	9 - 4 = 5	2 + 5 = 7
4 + 2 = 6	3 + 2 = 5	9 - 5 = 4	5 + 2 = 7
1 + 4 = 5	9 - 7 = 2	8 - 3 = 5	3 - 2 = 1
4 + 1 = 5	9 - 2 = 7	8 - 5 = 3	3 - 1 = 2

Multiplication Match

Directions: Cut out the multiplication number sentences at the bottom of the page. Glue them in the correct places in order to label the illustrated pictures.

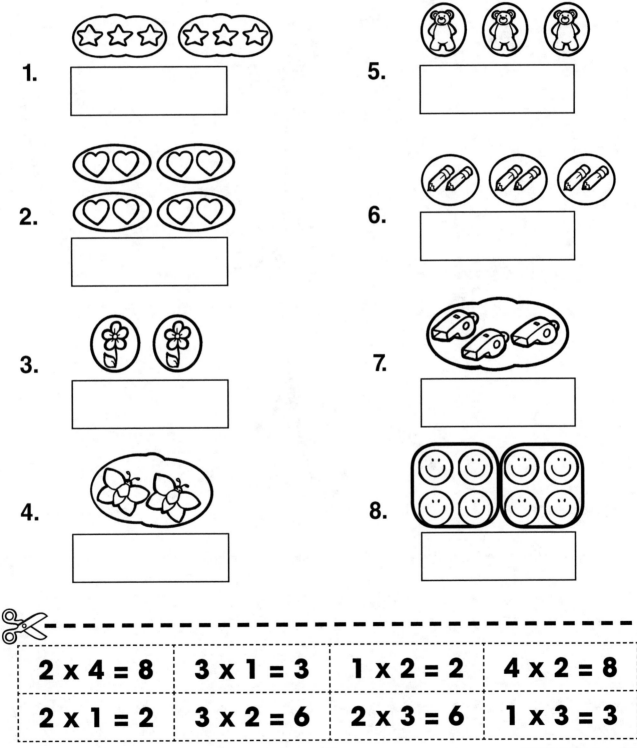

Same Product

Directions: Cut out the circles at the bottom of the page. Glue the multiplication problems on the butterfly according to the product.

Box It

Directions: Cut out the graph paper on page 48 into strips that illustrate the problems below. Glue the strips in the boxes. The first one is done for you.

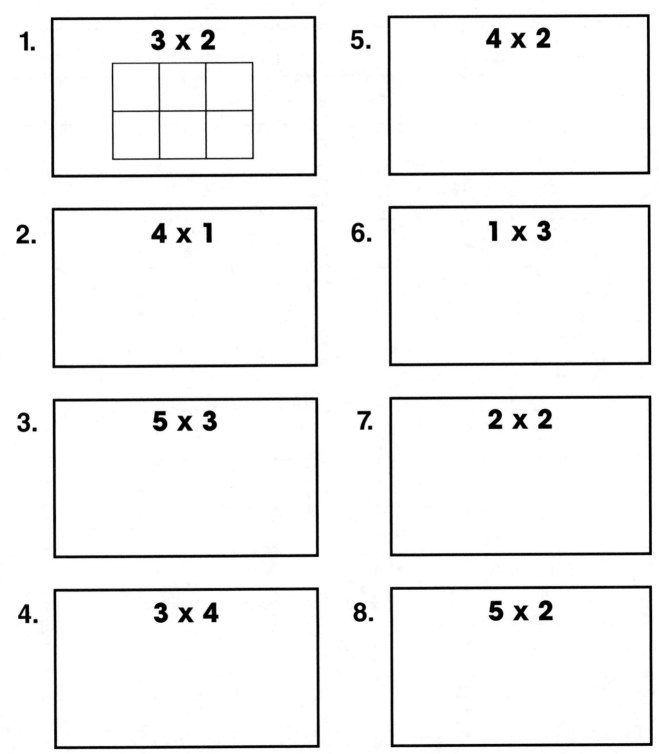

1. **3 x 2**

2. **4 x 1**

3. **5 x 3**

4. **3 x 4**

5. **4 x 2**

6. **1 x 3**

7. **2 x 2**

8. **5 x 2**

Graph Paper

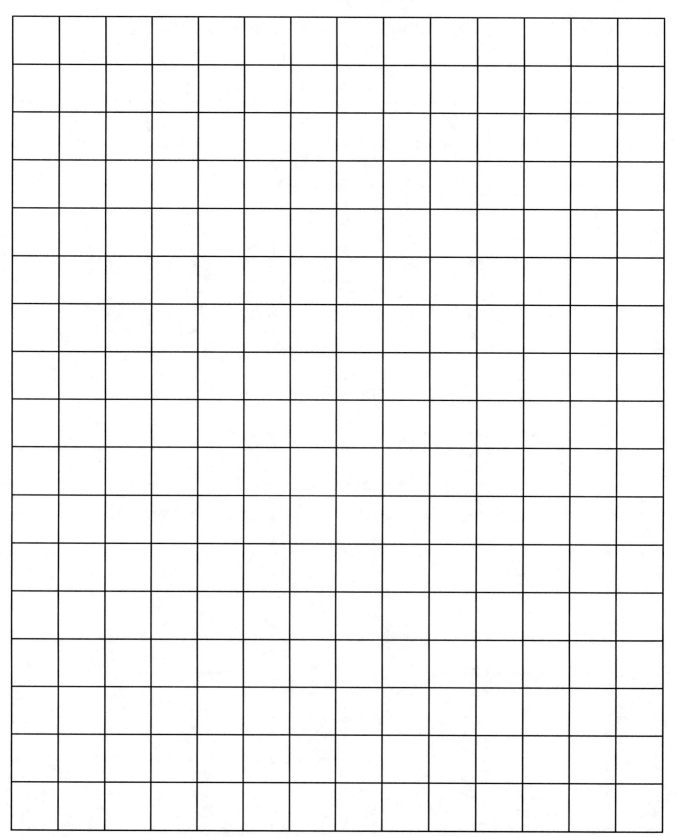

48

How Many?

Directions: Cut out the multiplication problems at the bottom of the page. Glue them in the correct places in order to provide a number sentence for the word problems. Write the product on the line provided.

1. How many eggs in 2 dozen? [   ] = _____

2. 8 kids took off their shoes. How many shoes are there? [   ] = _____

3. 2 kids rode their tricycles. How many wheels are there? [   ] = _____

4. 3 dogs went for a walk. How many dog legs are there? [   ] = _____

5. How many sides are on 6 triangles? [   ] = _____

6. 5 boys wear hats. How many hats are there? [   ] = _____

7. How many fingers on 2 hands? [   ] = _____

8. How many points on 3 stars? [   ] = _____

9. How many sides on 4 circles? [   ] = _____

10. How many knees on 6 girls? [   ] = _____

✂ -

0 x 4	2 x 3	5 x 1	8 x 2	6 x 2
2 x 5	3 x 4	2 x 12	6 x 3	3 x 5

Multiply It

Directions: Cut out the number word cards at the bottom of the page. Glue the word cards in the sentences below. Then, write a multiplication problem to correspond with the word problem. Be sure to include the product.

1. A mother with [＿＿＿＿] children wants to buy each of them [＿＿＿＿] new shirts. How many shirts will she buy? ＿＿＿ x ＿＿＿ = ＿＿＿

2. Mark wants to give [＿＿＿＿] friends each [＿＿＿＿] cookies. How many cookies will Mark need? ＿＿＿ x ＿＿＿ = ＿＿＿

3. Maria drank [＿＿＿＿] glasses of water every day for [＿＿＿＿] days. How many glasses of water did she drink? ＿＿＿ x ＿＿＿ = ＿＿＿

4. A recipe calls for [＿＿＿＿] cups of flour. We will make the recipe [＿＿＿＿] times. How many cups of flour will be needed? ＿＿＿ x ＿＿＿ = ＿＿＿

✂ -

two	**two**	**four**	**four**
three	**three**	**five**	**five**

The Duck Pond

Directions: Cut out the duck pictures at the bottom of the page. Glue some or all of the ducks in the picture in various places. Make up a math word problem to go with the picture. Solve the problem by showing your number sentence.

Cats

Directions: Cut out the cat pictures at the bottom of the page. Glue some or all of the cats in the picture in various places. Make up a math word problem to go with the picture. Solve the problem by showing your number sentence.

_____

_____

_____

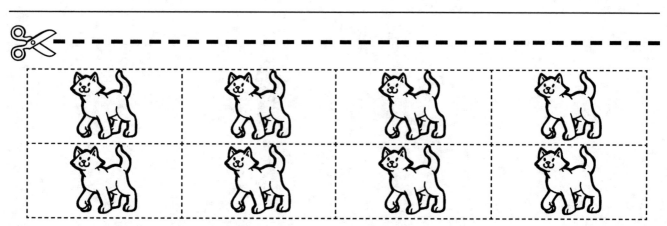

The Neighborhood

Directions: Cut out the car pictures at the bottom of the page. Glue some or all of the cars in the picture in various places. Make up a math word problem to go with the picture. Solve the problem by showing your number sentence.

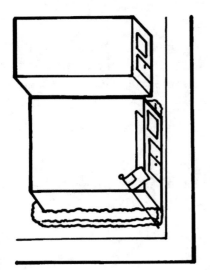 

Measurement

Suggested Activities

Below are suggested activities that can be used throughout the unit of study.

- Reproduce the clock pattern on pages 56 and 57 on index paper. Help students assemble the clock. Then, use the clocks as students practice telling time.

- Post your schedule each day on the board. Write the approximate time that each activity will take place or subject will be taught. Next to the time, draw a picture of what the clock will look like at that time. Students will begin to get used to seeing the written time and clock time together.

- Encourage parents to purchase inexpensive watches for their children. Children are always excited to have their own watch. It makes them feel grown up and promotes an immediate and motivating need to learn how to tell time.

- Help students create a step-by-step book of their daily schedule. Follow the directions below to create a step-by-step book. Have students keep a diary of one morning's events and write a different time and event on each page.

Materials
- four 9" x 12" (23 cm x 30 cm) sheets of construction paper
- long-arm stapler
- marking pens
- crayons
- colored pencils

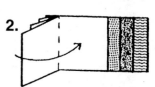

Directions
1. Have students place the four sheets of paper on top of one another, overlapping the ends.
2. Direct the students to hold the pages together and fold the pages over to create four more overlapping pages.
3. Help students staple the inside fold, and fold the pages back down.
4. Have students write the book title on the top page and write story sentences and illustrations on each succeeding page.

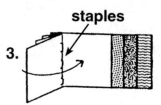

- Encourage students to become familiar with calendars by making a calendar for the entire year. This activity makes a great holiday gift for parents at Christmas, Hanukkah, Mother's Day, etc. Reproduce the calendar patterns on pages 63 and 64. Have students create a calendar for each month of the year. You will probably want to spread this activity out over several days, if not weeks. Glue each calendar on the bottom half of a 12" x 18" (30 cm x 46 cm) piece of construction paper. Collect art projects created throughout the school year to glue at the top of each piece of construction paper. Create a cover and bind the calendar pages together in the correct order. Students will have had a meaningful experience working with calendars, dates, and months, and they will also have a great gift to give to their parents!

Measurement *(cont.)*

Suggested Activities *(cont.)*

- Provide 3" x 5" (8 cm x 13 cm) index cards for students and a clock stamp. Clock stamps can be purchased at teacher supply stores. On one side of the index card, students write a digital time. On the other side of the index card, students stamp an image of the clock and then use a marker or a pencil to draw the hands on the clock. After the activity has been completed and checked by an adult, the index cards can be used as flashcards for students to practice telling the time.

- Gather a variety of measuring tools such as calendars, thermometers, clocks, scales, tape measure, rulers, etc. Place the measurement tools along with a variety of objects in a learning center. Allow students to experiment with using the tools even before you begin teaching the students how to use them. After you have taught the students to use the various measuring tools, place a "special" object in the center every week. Students must use all of the measuring tools they can in order to measure the object. For example, if you place an apple in the center, students could measure the circumference with a tape measure, the height, and the weight.

- Food is always a great motivator. Use holiday appropriate food or candy as non-standard units of measurement. For example, at Halloween, have students practice measuring using candy corns. Around Valentine's Day, have students practice measuring using candy hearts.

- Divide students into groups. Provide each group an object. Direct the students to go around the room and find three things that are longer than their groups' object. Then, direct them to find three things that are shorter than the object. Continue in a similar manner having the groups locate things that weigh more and less than their objects.

- Provide magazines for students to look through. Have the students cut a picture out of the magazine that they want to use for measurement practice. Students can then glue their picture to a piece of paper and then measure the objects in the pictures. Have students write the measurement below each picture. Students can do this activity practicing with a centimeter ruler, inches ruler, or both! This activity can also be adapted for weight. Since students will not be able to weigh the actual objects in the picture, have them sort the objects for items that weigh more than one pound and less than one pound.

- Have students bring their favorite stuffed animal from home. The first step is to have students draw a picture of their animal. Then, students should measure the various parts of the animal. For example, if the object is a teddy bear, students can measure the total height of the bear, the legs, etc. Students should write the measurements on the picture that they drew. The children can exchange animals and measure a friend's animal, too. Then students can compare to see if they got the same answers.

Make Your Own Clock

Directions: Cut out the pieces on this page and the next. Glue the circle together by putting glue on the tab and laying the half-circle from the next page on top of the tab. Glue the numbers on the clock in the correct places. Use a brad in order to attach the clock hands. Use the clock as you learn about telling time.

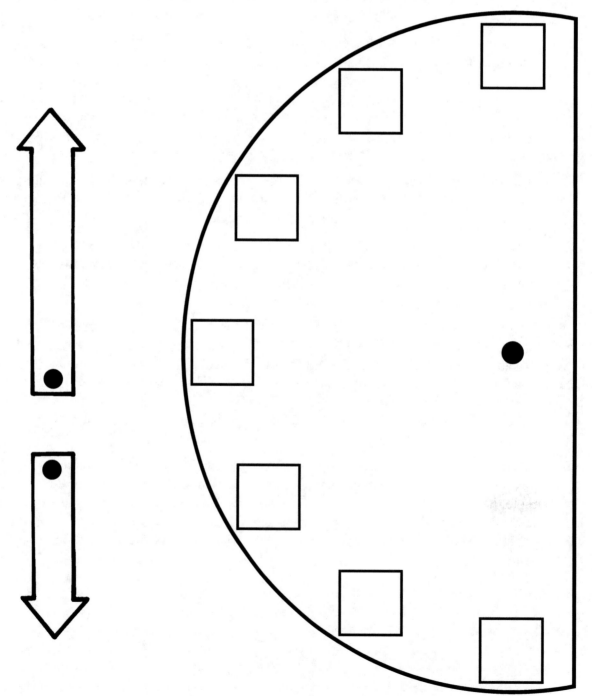

Make Your Own Clock *(cont.)*

1	2	3	4	5	6
7	8	9	10	11	12

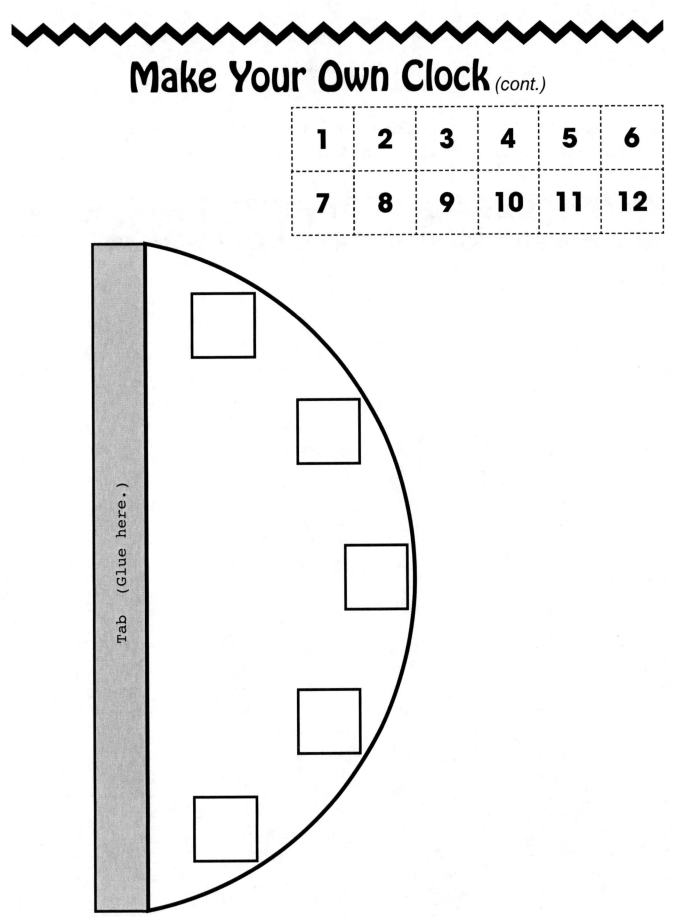

Tab (Glue here.)

Second, Minute, or Hour

Directions: Cut out the picture/word cards at the bottom of the page. Decide whether each activity would take a few seconds, a few minutes, or a few hours to complete. Glue the cards in the correct columns.

A Few Seconds	A Few Minutes	A Few Hours

go on a hike

do a jumping jack

sing a song

brush your teeth

your day at school

count to 10

go on a long drive

tie your shoes

write your name

Simone

write a letter to grandma

watch a movie

eat breakfast

On the Hour

Directions: Cut out the time cards at the bottom of the page. Look at the clocks below. Glue the correct time card under the clock showing that time.

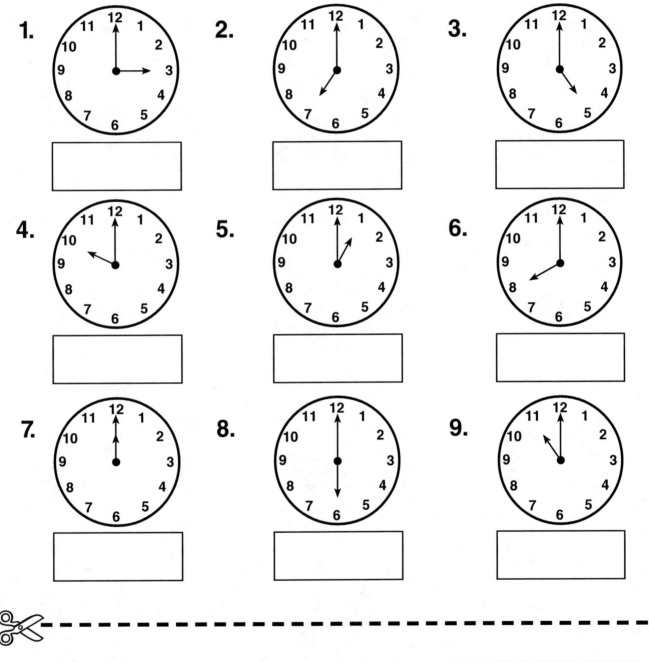

On the Half Hour

Directions: Cut out the clock faces at the bottom of the page. Glue them below in order to correctly show the time with a clock.

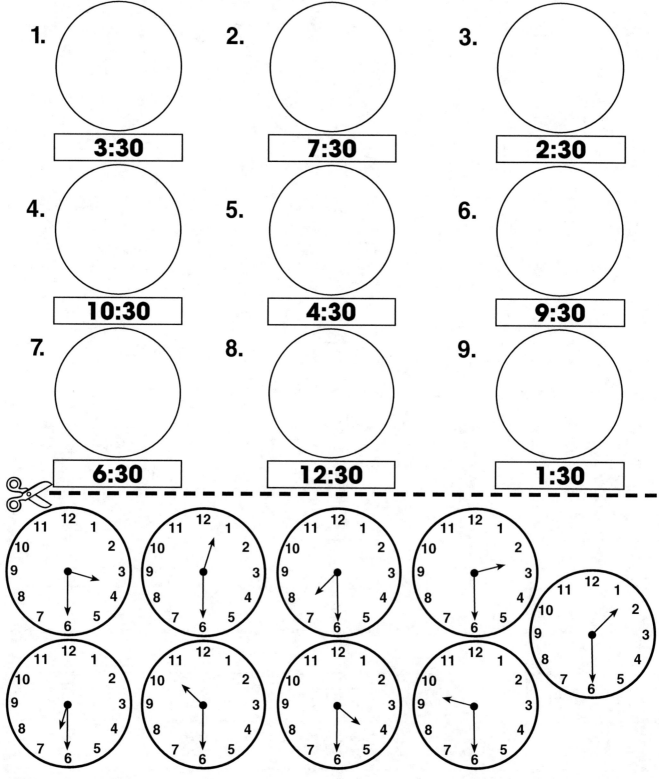

1. **3:30**

2. **7:30**

3. **2:30**

4. **10:30**

5. **4:30**

6. **9:30**

7. **6:30**

8. **12:30**

9. **1:30**

To the Minute

Directions: Cut out the time cards at the bottom of the page. Glue the time cards under the clocks in the correct places in order to show the time.

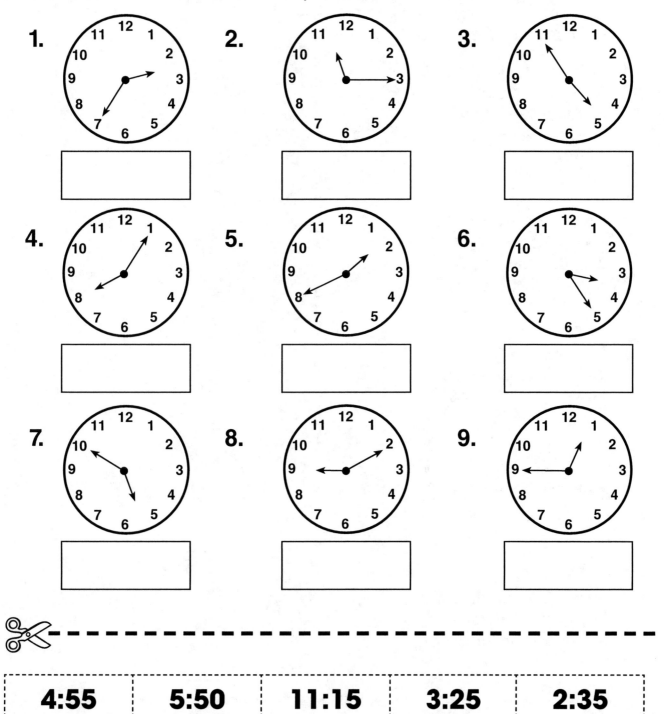

How Much Time?

Directions: Read the word problems. Draw the starting and ending times in the clock faces. Then cut out the word cards at the bottom of the page. Figure out how much time has elapsed in each problem. Glue the word card next to the problem in order to show an answer.

1. School starts at 8:00. School is done at 3:00. How many hours are children at school?

2. Mrs. Beemer teaches math from 9:00 to 10:30. How much time is math class?

3. Recess starts at 10:30 and ends at 11:00. How long is recess?

4. Band class meets from 11:00 to 12:00. How long is band?

5. Lunch starts at 12:30 and ends at 1:15. How long is lunch?

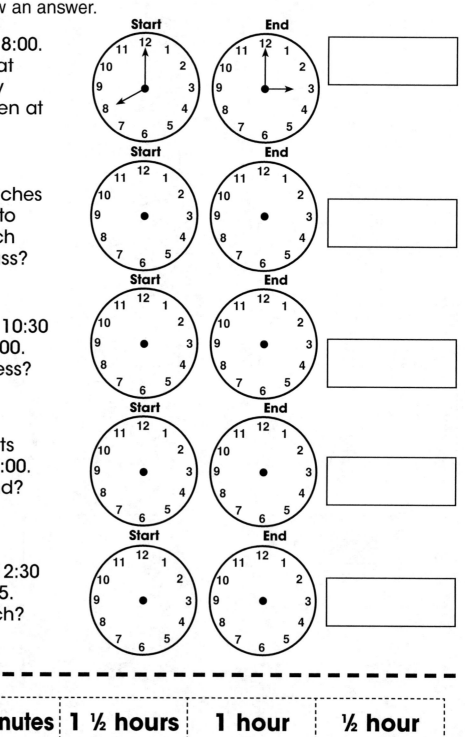

7 hours	45 minutes	1 ½ hours	1 hour	½ hour

Make Your Own Calendar

Directions: Photocopy the calendar on page 64. Cut out the pieces on page 63 in order to make your own calendar. Make the calendar for just this month or for the entire year. Use the words to label the month, days of the week, and the season. Then, write the numbers on the calendar to show the date. Use the holiday/special day squares to mark any special days that are in the month for which you are creating the calendar.

January
February
March
April
May
June
July
August
September
October
November
December

Sunday	Monday	Tuesday
Wednesday	Thursday	Friday
Saturday		

1st Day of School	Hanukkah	Easter	Last Day of School	New Years	Memorial Day
Picture Day	Veterans Day	4th of July	Field Trip	Lincoln's Birthday	Birthday
Labor Day	Washington	Winter	Halloween	Valentines Day	Spring
Thanksgiving	Martin Luther King	Summer	Christmas	St. Patrick's	Fall

Make Your Own Calendar *(cont.)*

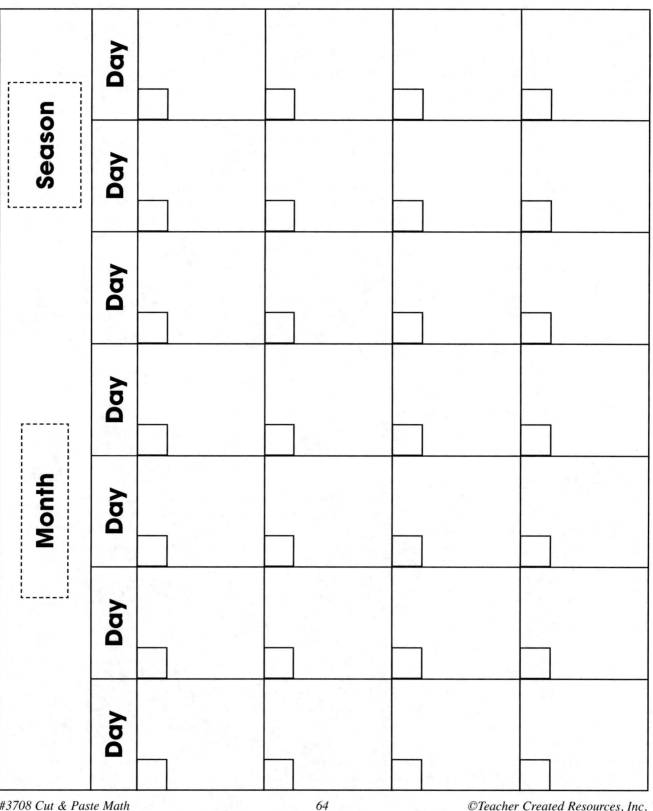

Shortest to Longest

Directions: Cut out the pieces at the bottom of the page. Glue the pieces in the correct boxes by object from shortest to longest.

1.

2.

3.

✂ --

Short to Tall

Directions: Cut out the picture cards at the bottom of the page. Sort the pictures by animals and people. Then, glue the picture cards in order from shortest to the tallest.

People

shortest ➝ ➝ ➝ ➝ ➝ ➝ **tallest**

Animals

shortest ➝ ➝ ➝ ➝ ➝ ➝ **tallest**

✂ —

Inch Worms

Directions: Cut out the ruler and the worm picture cards at the bottom of the page. Use the ruler to measure the worms. Glue the worms next to the correct measurement.

1. 2 inches

2. 5 inches

3. 1 inch

4. 6 inches

5. 4 inches

6. 3 inches

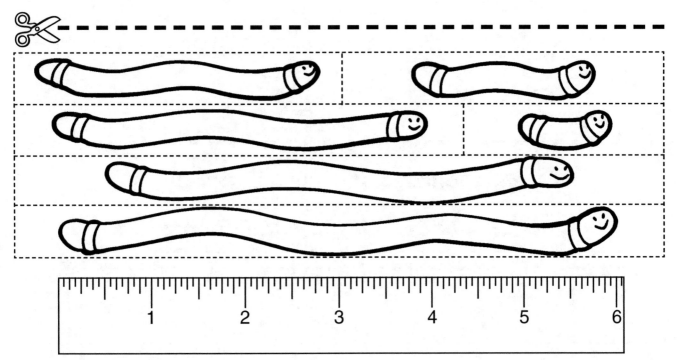

Measure It

Directions: Cut out the cards and ruler at the bottom of the page. Use the ruler to measure each line. Then, glue the correct measurement next to the line.

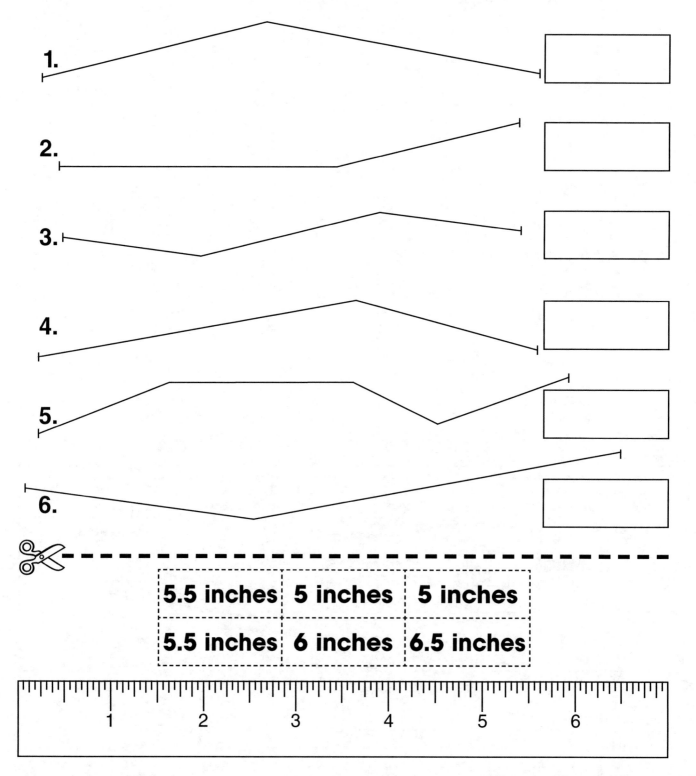

Grow a Garden

Directions: Cut out the ruler and the plants at the bottom of the page. Use the ruler to measure the plants. Glue the plants in the garden above the correct height.

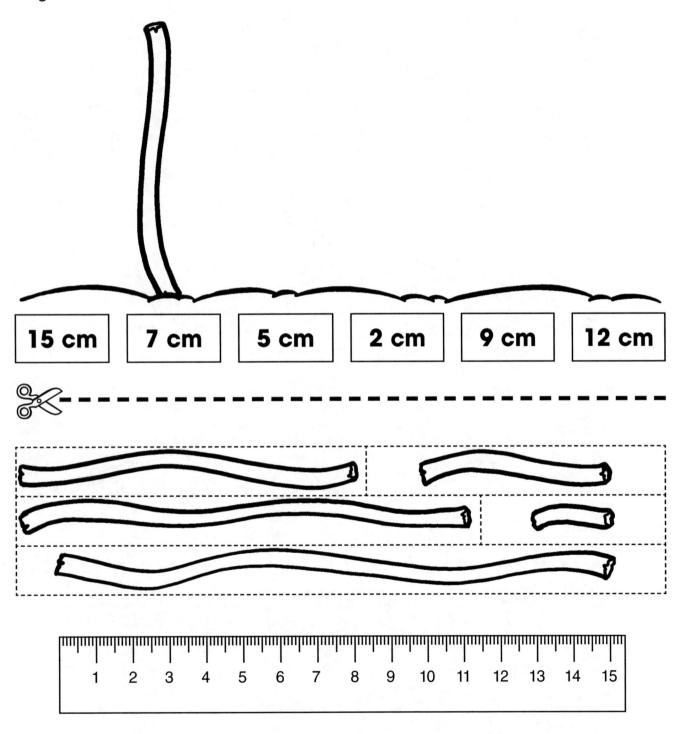

| 15 cm | 7 cm | 5 cm | 2 cm | 9 cm | 12 cm |

Which Weighs More?

Directions: Cut out the picture cards at the bottom of the page. Glue the picture cards on the balances below to show objects that are heavier and objects that are lighter.

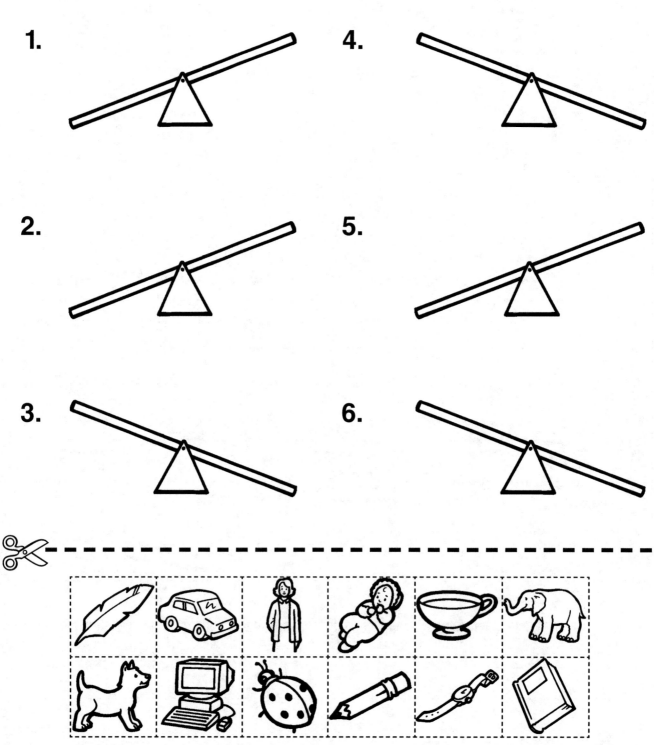

1.

2.

3.

4.

5.

6.

More or Less

Directions: Cut out the picture cards at the bottom of the page. Decide if the object in each picture weighs more or less than a pound. Glue the picture cards in the correct column.

More Than One Pound	Less Than One Pound

✂ --

Measurement Tools

Directions: Cut out the word and picture cards at the bottom of the page. Read each riddle. Glue a word card in order to answer each riddle. Glue the picture of the measurement tool next to each riddle.

1. I am used to show the date.
   What am I? I am a _____.

2. I am used to show how much something
   weighs. What am I? I am a _____.

3. I am used to check length and height.
   What am I? I am a _____.

4. I am used to tell time. What am I?
   I am a _____.

5. I am used to show volume. What am I?
   I am a _____.

✂ -

| calendar | clock | ruler | scale | cup |

Geometry

Suggested Activities

Below are suggested activities that can be used throughout the unit of study.

- Divide a large sheet of butcher paper into four sections. Label each section with the name of a shape: square, circle, triangle, and rectangle. Then, have students look through magazines to find examples of each shape. Students should cut out their examples and glue them on the piece of butcher paper in the correct section in order to illustrate each shape. Additional sections can be added for other shapes being studied such as octagon or even solid shapes.

- Show students how to break down objects that they want to draw into shapes. Conduct some guided drawing sessions in order to demonstrate this technique to students. Be sure to use the names of the shapes as you guide students through drawing. You will see a definite improvement in their artistic abilities.

- Provide students with a given number of shapes. For example, provide them with 4 triangles, 3 squares, 6 circles, and 2 rectangles. You may even wish to use pattern blocks for this activity. Challenge students to create an object using the shapes. If you use paper versions of the shapes, you can have the students glue their picture down onto a piece of construction paper. This picture can be used as the basis for a writing project too, or you can simply have the students identify how many of each shape were used.

- Create Venn diagrams comparing and contrasting two shapes (or more!). Compare and contrast features such as the number of corners, the number of sides, the size of the sides, the sizes of the shapes drawn on the Venn diagram, etc. Post the Venn diagrams in the room.

- Use pretzel sticks to help students practice making and identifying shapes. Provide each student a napkin or a piece of construction paper and a handful of pretzel sticks. Call out a shape you want students to make. Students then use their pretzel sticks to create the shape. The best part about this project is that you can eat it when you are finished!

- Have students go on a scavenger hunt at their houses looking for solid shapes. Divide a piece of paper into sections. Label each section with the solid shape and a drawing of the shape that you want students to look for. Students must write down any object they find in their houses that comes in that shape. For example, under cylinder, students could write "cat food can," "soup can," and "ice cream container." Challenge students to find as many examples of each solid shape as possible. You may even want to give a prize out to the student who finds the most.

- Have students create solid shapes out of toothpicks and mini marshmallows. The marshmallows become the corners when students poke toothpicks into them. Challenge students to make a model of as many of the solid shapes studied as they can.

Geometry *(cont.)*

Suggested Activities *(cont.)*

- Discuss with students various places symmetry occurs in nature, including on butterfly wings. Then, create this beautiful butterfly art project to illustrate symmetry. Line a desk with newspaper. Provide a variety of colors of liquid tempera paint from which the students can choose. Fold a piece of white, 9" x 12" (23 cm x 30 cm) construction paper in half, one for each student. Open the folded paper so that it lays flat on the desk. Have each child choose 3–5 paint colors that he or she will use on his or her butterfly. Students should squeeze approximately 10 drops of the tempera paint colors they chose on only one half of the construction paper. The drops should be about the side of a dime. Once the paint has been applied, gently fold the side of the construction paper with no paint over, so that it touches the paint. Use your hand to gently press on the folded paper. Unfold the paper to reveal a symmetrical design. Allow the paper to dry thoroughly. Once dry, fold the paper in half again and cut the shape of a butterfly. It is fun to use the scissors that cut special designs. Add pipe cleaners for antennae. Display the butterflies on a bulletin board with a title or explanation card of how these beautiful butterflies illustrate a mathematical and natural concept.

- Provide each child with a piece of white, 9" x 12" (23 cm x 30 cm) construction paper and two different colored pieces of 4" x 6" (10 cm x 15 cm) construction paper. First, have students use one of the 4" x 6" (10 cm x 15 cm) construction paper pieces to cut a random design. Then, demonstrate to students how they can create a symmetrical design by folding the other piece of 4" x 6" (10 cm x 15 cm) construction paper in half. Show them how to hold the "fold" side of the paper in one hand and use their other hand to cut a design. Students should then glue the symmetrical and non-symmetrical design on the larger piece of construction paper. Have them label each design as "Symmetrical" or "Not Symmetrical." You may also wish to have students draw a dotted line on their symmetrical design to show the line of symmetry.

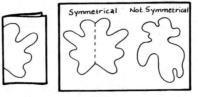

- Fold a piece of 8 1/2" x 11" (22 cm x 28 cm) paper in half. On one half of the paper have students draw half of a figure or even just a doodle. Then, have the students trade papers with one another. Students must complete the picture by making the drawing symmetrical.

- Have students analyze numbers and letters of the alphabet for symmetry. Create a chart that shows which numbers and letters are symmetrical and which are not.

Shape Match

Directions: Cut out the shapes at the bottom of the page. Glue them in the correct box.

Triangles △	Squares ☐
Circles ○	**Rectangles** ▭

✂ –

Shape Riddles

Directions: Cut out the shapes and word cards at the bottom of the page. Read the riddles below. Glue the word cards in place to correctly complete each sentence. Glue the shape next to the riddle to illustrate it.

1. I have 4 corners. I have 4 sides.
   All of my sides are equal.
   What am I?

   I am a ⬚.

2. I do not have any corners. I am round all around.
   My sides are curved.
   What am I?

   I am a ⬚.

3. I have 3 corners. I have 3 sides.
   What am I?

   I am a ⬚.

4. I have 4 sides. Two sides are short,
   two sides are long. What am I?

   I am a ⬚.

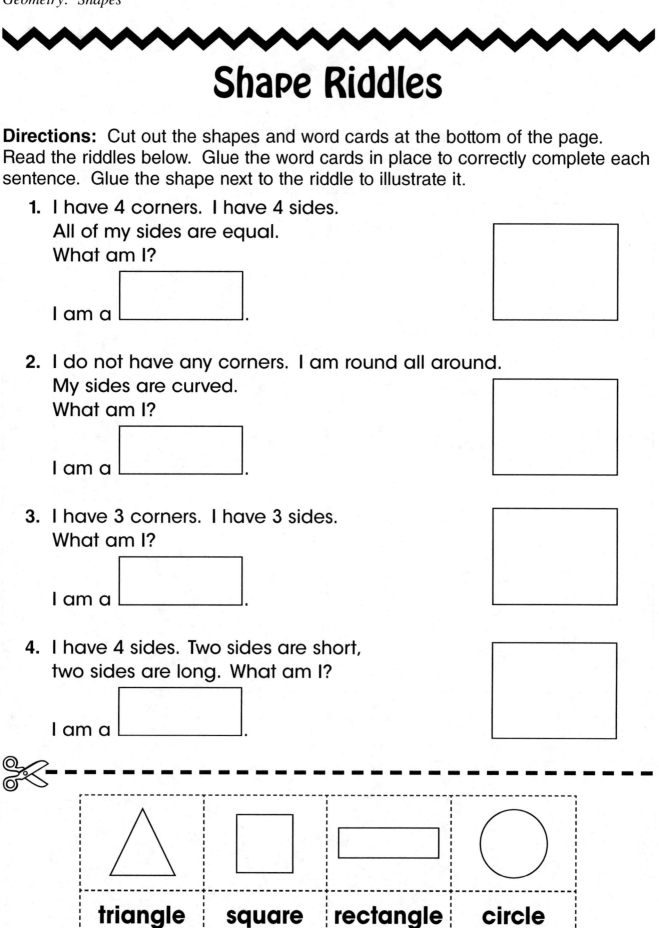

triangle : **square** : **rectangle** : **circle**

Blast Off

Directions: Color and cut out the shapes at the bottom of the page. Glue the shapes in place to create a space ship like the one shown. Then, answer the questions.

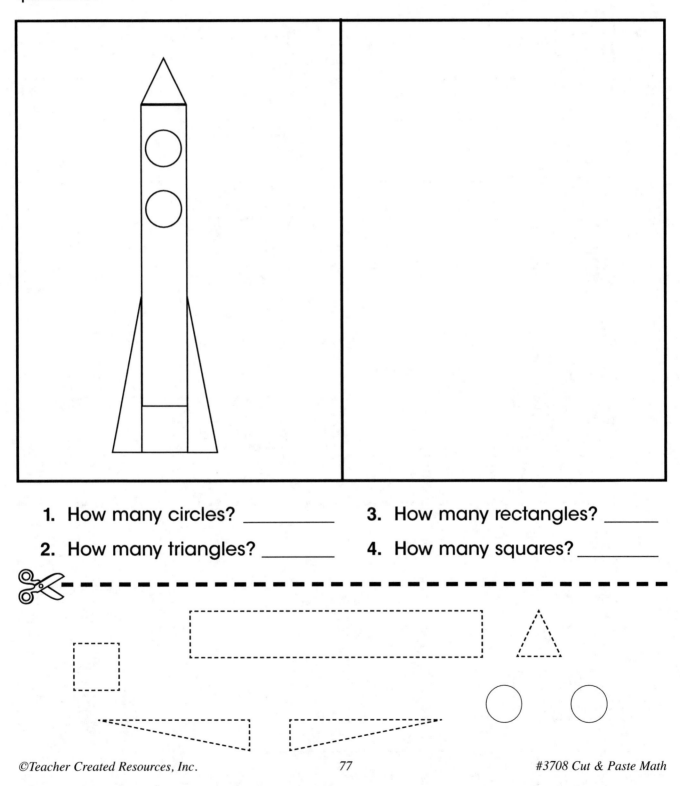

1. How many circles? _____   3. How many rectangles? _____

2. How many triangles? _____   4. How many squares? _____

Three-Dimensional Shapes

Directions: Cut out the word cards below. Glue the cards in the correct places in order to label the shapes of the objects.

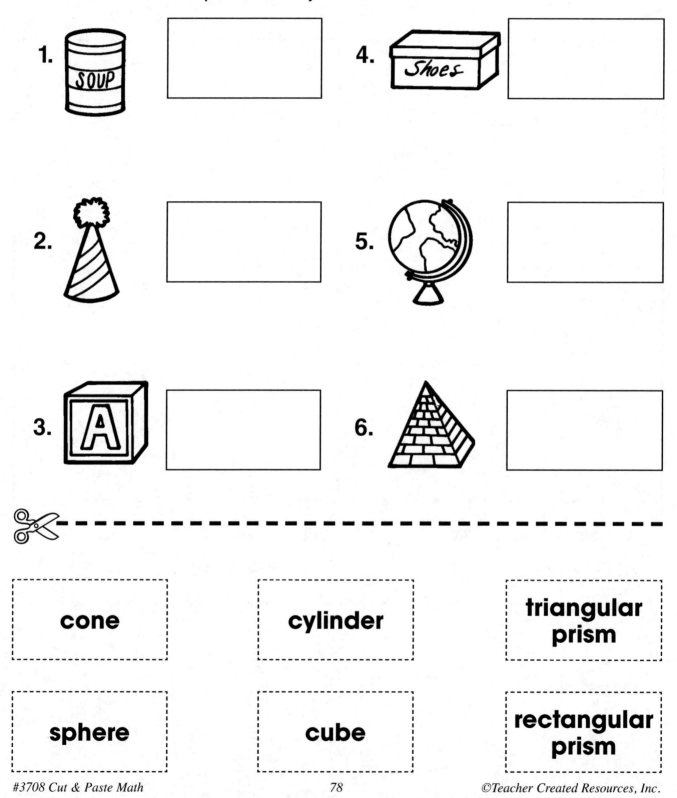

1.

4.

2.

5.

3.

6.

| cone | cylinder | triangular prism |

| sphere | cube | rectangular prism |

Which Shape?

Directions: Cut out the objects below. Glue the picture next to the correct shape of the object.

sphere	
cylinder	
cube	
rectangular prism	
cone	

Roll or Stack?

Directions: Cut out the solids at the bottom of the page. Glue the solids in the correct column to show if the shapes will roll or stack.

Roll	Stack

✂ -

Make It Whole

Directions: Cut out the picture cards at the bottom of the page. Glue the picture cards in the correct places in order to make symmetrical figures.

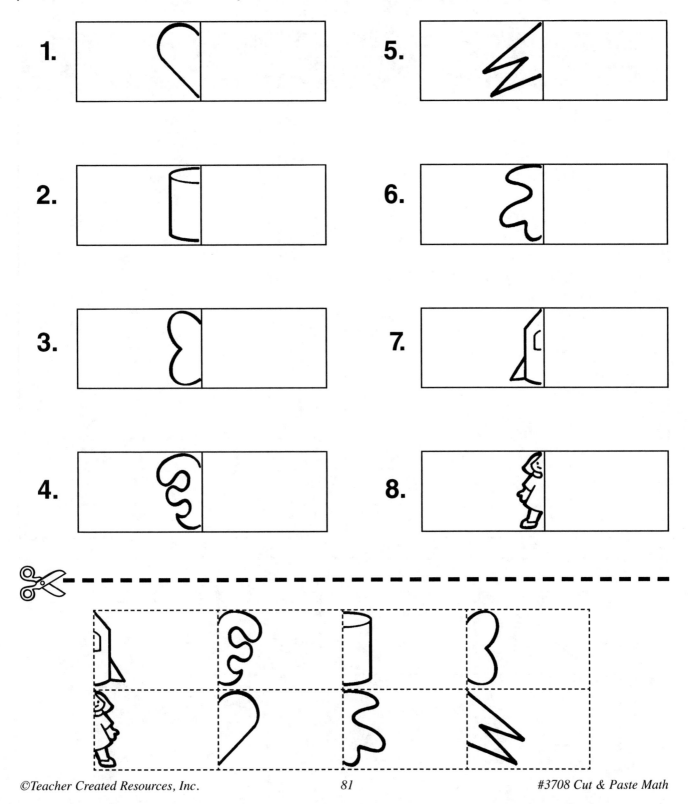

Symmetrical or Not

Directions: Cut out the shape cards at the bottom of the page. Glue the shapes in the correct column in order to show if the shapes are symmetrical or not symmetrical.

Symmetrical	Not Symmetrical

Congruent Shapes

Directions: Cut out the shape cards at the bottom of the page. Glue the shapes that are congruent to the shapes shown below in the same row. Discard any shapes that are not congruent.

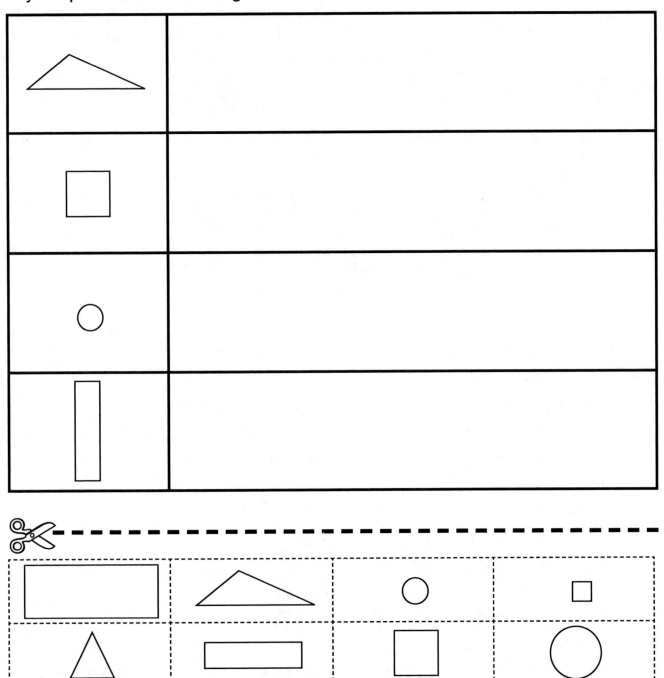

Organizing and Presenting Data

Suggested Activities

Below are suggested activities that can be used throughout the unit of study.

- Show students how their hand can be a model of tally marks. Write the number one on the chalkboard. Show students how to hold up one finger to represent one. Then, show students one tally mark on the board. Continue writing down numbers, holding up fingers, and making tally marks through four. When you get to five, show students how to fold their four fingers down into their palms and cross the fingers with their thumb. Their hand should be in the shape of a fist. Demonstrate how the fifth tally mark crosses the first four on the chalkboard.

- Use tally marks to practice counting by fives. Make tally marks whenever you have to keep track of numbers so that students become accustom to seeing how the tally marks can be used. Have students make their own tally marks as you ask them questions. You can simply ask the question orally or write it on the board. Provide the choices written on the board. Then, students have to form a line. Each child places his or her tally mark under the answer he/she is providing. Then, have the class find totals for each response by counting the tallies. For example, you can take the lunch count this way by having students mark whether they will be buying their lunches or if they brought their lunches. Use tallies to record students' predictions, too. For example, "Do you think Felix's loose tooth will fall out before lunch or after lunch?"

- Graphs are great for documenting student ideas and favorite things. Graphs where students give input provide an authentic way to learn about graphing. You can create simple graphs to which students must respond every day. The graphs can be made out of paper. Consider graphing some of these examples.

What is your favorite food?	Where did you go on summer vacation?
What is your favorite color?	Have you ever been to the beach?
What is your favorite TV show?	How do you get to school?
What is your favorite subject?	Are you going to buy your lunch or did you bring it from home?
What is your favorite game?	
What is your favorite sport?	How many food groups were represented in your lunch?
What is your favorite holiday?	
What is your favorite number?	Have you ever visited another state/country/continent?
What is your favorite toy?	Do you speak another language?
What color are your eyes?	Which version of Cinderella did you like best?
How many people are in your family?	Which apple did you like best? (after a taste test)
What do you like to do when it is raining?	Do you like to take a bath?
What time do you go to bed?	Have you ever held a snake?

Creating and Presenting Data *(cont.)*

Suggested Activities *(cont.)*

Try some of these ideas for creating graphs:

- Create a clothespin graph that can be used for questions for which students will only have two options. Write each child's name on both sides of a clothespin. Then, laminate a piece of tagboard for durability. You can use a whiteboard marker on lamination and erase it with a whiteboard eraser. Write a question at the top of the tag and then provide two responses from which students may choose, one on each half of the tagboard. Students must clip their clothespin on the tagboard on the side to which they will be responding. Students can read the graph by counting how many each side has, which side has more/less, how many more one side has over the other, etc.

- Use magnets on a magnetic surface (such as most whiteboards). Provide a small magnet for each student with his or her name on it. Then, all you have to do is write a question on the board and have students place their magnets under/next to their responses.

- Paper graphs work well, too. Use a large sheet of butcher paper and create the graph on the butcher paper. Students can come up to vote/respond to the question at the top of the piece of butcher paper. You may wish to have students respond with a colored dot sticker, by writing their names on white labels and sticking the labels to the butcher paper, by gluing a symbol (such as a bear shape) on the graph, or by simply having them color a square. Create the graph at the top part of the piece of butcher paper. Be sure to tear some extra butcher paper so that you will have space at the bottom of the graph to record student observations when reading the graph.

- Creating flip books provides a great visual for students to see the number of possibilities there are for a situation. For example, if students wanted to find out how many outfits can be made from 2 shirts and 2 pairs of pants, provide a picture of a child wearing a shirt and pants (or you can have the students create their own). First, students color the shirts and pants the different colors. Then, have the students staple the pages together to form a book. Be sure the pages are lined up neatly. Then, cut along the pages until 1/2" (1.3 cm) from the left edge of the paper so that the pages can flip. Students can then flip the pages and record the various outfits that can be created.

Tallies

Directions: Cut out the number cards at the bottom of the page. Glue the numbers next to the tallies to show how many tally marks there are.

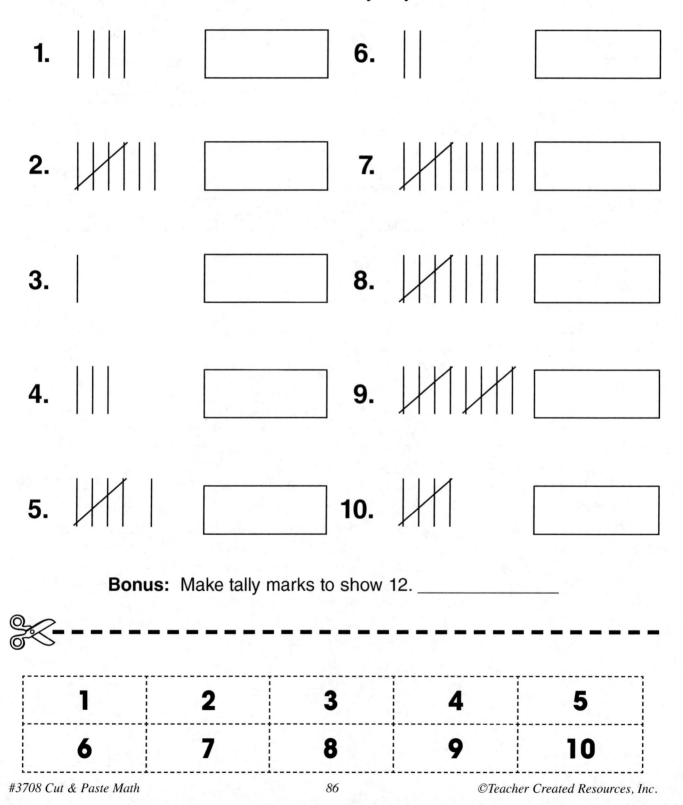

Bonus: Make tally marks to show 12. _____

| 1 | 2 | 3 | 4 | 5 |
| 6 | 7 | 8 | 9 | 10 |

86

How Many Tallies?

1. 7

2. 15

3. 30

4. 12

5. 23

6. 4

7. 1

8. 18

9. 9

10. 27

11. 25

12. 21

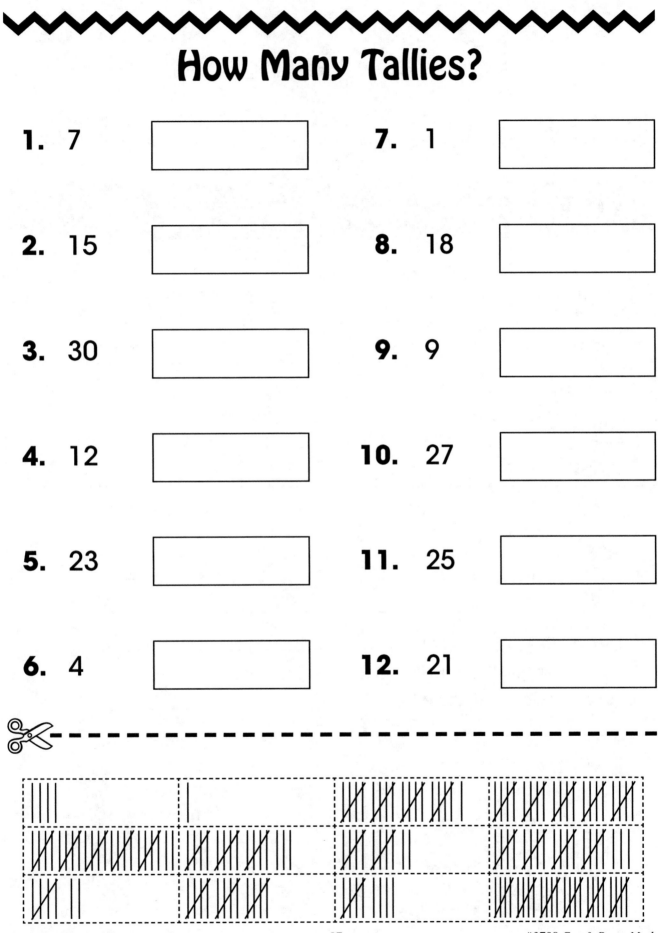

Pet Favorites

Directions: Create a graph to show people's favorite pets. Cut out the animal cards at the bottom of the page. Glue them in the correct places to complete the graph. Then, use the graph to answer the questions.

Favorite Pet	
Dog	
Cat	
Bird	

1. How many birds are there? _____

2. How many dogs are there? _____

3. How many cats are there? _____

Desserts

Directions: Create a graph to show people's favorite desserts. Cut out the dessert cards at the bottom of the page. Glue them in the correct places to complete the graph. Then, use the graph to answer the questions.

Favorite Desserts			
Pie	**Cake**	**Ice Cream**	**Cookies**

1. How many people like cake and ice cream? _____

2. How many more people like cake than pie? _____

3. How many people were surveyed in all? _____

Favorite Subject

Directions: Find out if your friends like reading, math, or science. First, interview six friends by asking them whether they like reading, math, or science best. Use tally marks to keep track of their responses. Then, cut out the symbols at the bottom of the page and use them to help you complete the graph below.

Reading	Math	Science
_____	_____	_____

Favorite Subjects

Reading	
Math	
Science	

✂ —

Make the Line

Directions: Cut out the figures at the bottom of the page. Read the clues in order to figure out where each person is standing in line. Then, glue the figures in place.

1st   **Last**

Clues

- Pei is in the middle.

- Miguel is at the front of the line.

- Justin is standing between Miguel and Pei.

- Marie is at the end of the line.

- Amy is standing in front of Marie.

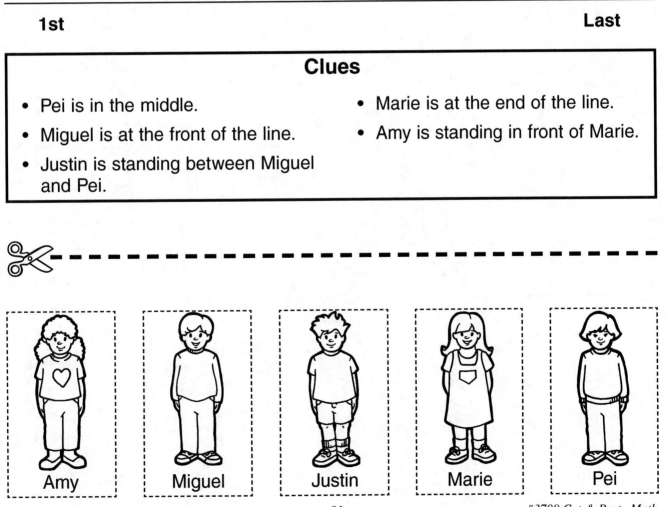

Amy   Miguel   Justin   Marie   Pei

Making Outfits

Directions: How many outfits can you make with two shirts and two pairs of shorts? That is your job! Figure out how many different outfits you can make with a red shirt, a blue shirt, green shorts, and orange shorts. Begin by coloring the clothing the colors that are written on them. Cut out the clothing at the bottom of the page. Glue the shirts and shorts on the boy below to make different outfits.

Answer Key

Page 6
1. four
2. zero
3. three
4. five
5. two
6. one
7. eight
8. seven

Page 7
1. three
2. five
3. six
4. one
5. zero
6. two
7. eight
8. nine

Page 8
Top row: 1, one; 5, five
Middle row: 4, four; 2, two
Bottom row: 3, three; 6, six

Page 9
1. three
2. two
3. one
4. zero
5. six
6. four
7. seven
8. five

Page 10
Top row: fifteen, twenty, twelve, eighteen
Middle row: eleven, nineteen, thirteen
Bottom row: fourteen, sixteen, seventeen

Page 11
1. second
2. fifth
3. sixth
4. third
5. fourth
6. first

Page 12

1st 2nd 3rd 4th 5th

6th 7th 8th 9th 10th

Page 13
1. first
2. fifth
3. second
4. third
5. fourth
6. sixth

Page 14
sixth, first, fourth, fifth, second, third

Page 15
(10), 20, (30), 40, (50), 60, (70), 80, (90), 100

Page 16
5, 10
15, 20
25, 30
35, 40
45, 50
55, 60
65, 70
75, 80
85, 90
95, 100

Page 17
(2), 4, 6, (8), 10
(12), 14, 16, 18, (20)
22, (24), 26, (28), 30
(32), 34, 36, 38, (40)

Page 18
1. 60, 80
2. 20, 30
3. 6, 12
4. 30, 50
5. 15, 35
6. 32, 38

Page 19
Accept all answers that make the statements true.

Page 20
1. <
2. >
3. =
4. <
5. <
6. =
7. >
8. <
9. =
10. >

Page 21
True
76 > 72, 91 > 89, 84 = 84, 63 < 67, 33 < 38, 43 > 36
False
21 > 28, 67 < 61, 82 < 79, 46 > 48, 49 > 51, 73 < 71

Page 22
1. 28
2. 44
3. 60
4. 71
5. 25
6. 33
7. 53
8. 75

Page 23
1. Pictures show 1 hundred, 2 tens, and 4 ones
2. Pictures show 2 hundreds, 3 tens, and 7 ones
3. Pictures show 2 hundreds, 4 tens, and 1 one
4. Pictures show 1 hundred, 7 tens, and 3 ones

Page 24
1. 496
2. 372
3. 148
4. 350
5. 209

Page 25
1. 2
2. 6
3. 5
4. 4
5. 3

Page 26
1. 1, 3
2. 4, 6
3. 6, 8
4. 2, 4
5. 3, 5
6. 0, 2
7. 5, 7
8. 7, 9

Answer Key (cont.)

Page 27
Ten More
(5), 15
(23), 33
(47), 57
(54), 64
(86), 96
(90), 100
Ten Less
(30), 20
(43), 33
(57), 47
(64), 54
(71), 61
(95), 85

Page 28
Accept all answers that show the given amount in coins.

Page 29
1. 14¢
2. 18¢
3. 12¢
4. 19¢
5. 10¢
6. 17¢

Page 30
1. $0.63
2. $1.25
3. $0.93
4. $0.45
5. $0.01
6. $1.45
7. $1.01
8. $0.55

Page 33
Accept all answers that illustrate the number sentence.
1. 3
2. 4
3. 5
4. 6
5. 7
6. 7

Page 34
5—5+0, 4+1, 3+2, 1+4, 0+5
6—6+0, 5+1, 3+3, 4+2, 1+5
7—7+0, 4+3, 2+5, 1+6, 3+4
8—8+0, 1+7, 2+6, 5+3, 4+4

Page 35
Answers will vary.

Page 36
1. 5
2. 6
3. 8
4. 8
5. 7
6. 9
7. 7
8. 6

Page 37
1. 77
2. 57
3. 65
4. 95
5. 89
6. 56
7. 85
8. 87

Page 38
1. 82
2. 81
3. 51
4. 74
5. 64
6. 90
7. 41
8. 95

Page 39
1. Picture showing five smiley faces with three crossed out.
2. Picture showing four pencils with one crossed out.
3. Picture showing two bears with two bears crossed out.
4. Picture showing three hearts.
5. Picture showing four stars with two stars crossed out.
6. Picture showing seven flowers with two crossed out.

Page 40
2: 7 – 5, 9 – 7, 6 – 4
3: 3 – 0, 4 – 1, 7 – 4
4: 8 – 4, 6 – 2, 5 – 1
5: 7 – 2, 5 – 0, 8 – 3

Page 41
1. 5 – 2 = 3
2. 7 – 3 = 4
3. 3 – 3 = 0
4. 6 – 2 = 4
5. 9 – 5 = 4
6. 4 – 3 = 1

Page 42
1. 56
2. 32
3. 21
4. 33
5. 41
6. 18
7. 12
8. 41

Page 43
1. 56
2. 19
3. 9
4. 18
5. 27
6. 39
7. 49
8. 7

Page 44
1. 3 – 2 = 1, 3 – 1 = 2
2. 1 + 4 = 5, 4 + 1 = 5
3. 2 + 3 = 5, 3 + 2 = 5
4. 9 – 7 = 2, 9 – 2 = 7
5. 2 + 5 = 7, 5 + 2 = 7
6. 8 – 3 = 5, 8 – 5 = 3
7. 9 – 4 = 5, 9 – 5 = 4
8. 2 + 4 = 6, 4 + 2 = 6

Page 45
1. 2 x 3 = 6
2. 4 x 2 = 8
3. 2 x 1 = 2
4. 1 x 2 = 2
5. 3 x 1 = 3
6. 3 x 2 = 6
7. 1 x 3 = 3
8. 2 x 4 = 8

Page 46
12: 3 x 4, 2 x 6, 4 x 3, 6 x 2
18: 3 x 6, 6 x 3, 9 x 2, 2 x 9
24: 8 x 3, 3 x 8, 6 x 4, 4 x 6
36: 36 x 1, 9 x 4, 4 x 9, 6 x 6

Answer Key (cont.)

Page 47
Illustrations can vary. Check to make sure illustrations match equation.

Page 49
1. 2 x 12 = 24
2. 8 x 2 = 16
3. 2 x 3 = 6
4. 3 x 4 = 12
5. 6 x 3 = 18
6. 5 x 1 = 5
7. 2 x 5 = 10
8. 3 x 5 = 15
9. 0 x 4 = 0
10. 6 x 2 =12

Page 50
Answers will vary.

Page 51
Answers will vary.

Page 52
Answers will vary.

Page 53
Answers will vary.

Page 58
A Few Seconds—do a jumping jack, count to 10, tie your shoes, write your name

A Few Minutes—sing a song, brush your teeth, write a letter to Grandma, eat breakfast

A Few Hours—go on a hike, your day at school, go on a long drive, watch a movie

Page 59
1. 3:00
2. 7:00
3. 5:00
4. 10:00
5. 1:00
6. 8:00
7. 12:00
8. 6:00
9. 11:00

Page 60

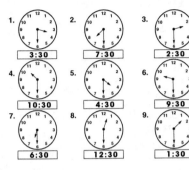

Page 61
1. 2:35
2. 11:15
3. 4:55
4. 8:05
5. 1:40
6. 3:25
7. 5:50
8. 9:10
9. 12:45

Page 62

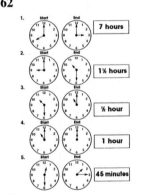

Page 65
Check to make sure illustrations are shortest to the longest.

Page 66
Check to make sure illustrations are from shortest to the tallest.

Page 67
Check to make sure illustrations match measurements.

Page 68
1. 5.5 inches
2. 5 inches
3. 5 inches
4. 5.5 inches
5. 6 inches
6. 6.5 inches

Page 69
Check to make sure illustrations match measurements.

Page 70
Answers will vary.

Page 71
More Than One Pound: cat, TV, dog, lamp, phone, chair
Less Than One Pound: ring, paper clip, penny, nail, strawberry, pencil

Page 72
1. calendar
2. scale
3. ruler
4. clock
5. cup

Page 75

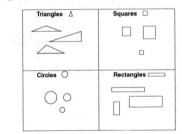

Page 76
1. square
2. circle
3. triangle
4. rectangle

Page 77
1. 2
2. 3
3. 1
4. 1

Page 78
1. cylinder
2. cone
3. cube
4. rectangular prism
5. sphere
6. triangular prism

Page 79
Sphere: basketball, globe
Cylinder: soup can, tuna can
Cube: file box, block
Rectangular Prism: book, shoebox
Cone: party hat, ice cream cone

Page 80

Roll: pencil, ball, marker

Stack: shoebox, block, book

Page 81

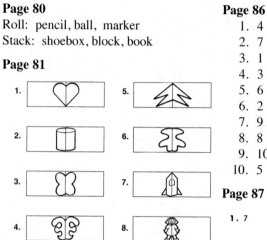

Page 82

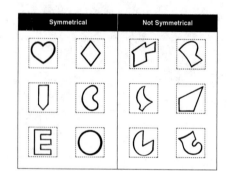

Page 83

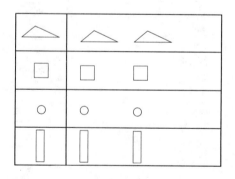

Page 86

1. 4
2. 7
3. 1
4. 3
5. 6
6. 2
7. 9
8. 8
9. 10
10. 5

Page 87

1. 7
2. 15
3. 30
4. 12
5. 23
6. 4
7. 1
8. 18
9. 9
10. 27
11. 25
12. 21

Page 88

1. 3
2. 4
3. 5

Page 89

1. 10
2. 1
3. 18

Page 90

Answers will vary.

Page 91

Miguel, Justin, Pei, Amy, Marie

Page 92

Outfit 1 – red shirt, green shorts

Outfit 2 – blue shirt, green shorts

Outfit 3 – red shirt, orange shorts

Outfit 4 – blue shirt, orange shorts